Walking Haunted London

Walking *Haunted London*

RICHARD JONES

TWENTY-FIVE ORIGINAL WALKS EXPLORING LONDON'S GHOSTLY PAST

NEW HOLLAND

This edition first published in 2004 by
New Holland Publishers (UK) Ltd
London • Cape Town • Sydney • Auckland

www.newhollandpublishers.com

Garfield House
86–88 Edgware Road
London W2 2EA
United Kingdom

80 McKenzie Street
Cape Town 8001
South Africa

14 Aquatic Drive
Frenchs Forest, NSW 2086
Australia

218 Lake Road
Northcote, Auckland
New Zealand

ISBN 1 84330 940 8

Publishing Manager: Jo Hemmings
Senior Editor: Kate Michell
Copy Editor: Ann Hildyard
Cartographer: ML Design
Designers: Behram Kapadia and Alan Marshall
Indexer: Raoul de Bunsen

Reproduction by Pica Colour Separation Overseas (Pte) Ltd, Singapore
Printed and bound in Singapore by Kyodo Printing Co (Singapore) Pte Ltd

Photographic Acknowledgements
All photographs by the author with the exception of the following:
Axiom Photographic Agency/Chris Parker: Plate 30; Chris Brackley: Plate 4; Andrew
Duncan: Plates 19, 20; Fergus Noone Photography: Plate 33; Fortean Picture Library:
Plate 8; Life File Photo Library/Andrew Ward: Plates 1, 2, 7, 9, 14, 21, 24, 25, 28; Oliver
Lim: Plate 10; London Tourist Board Slide Library: Plate 13; Mary Evans Picture Library:
Plates 3, 12, 23, 27, 29; Photobank/Michael Bailie: Plate 32; PictureBank Photo Library
Ltd: Plates 15, 16, 22, 31; William Smuts: Plate 11; Windsor Tourist Board: Plate 26

Front cover: Houses of Parliament, photographed by Andrew Ward for
Life File Photo Library

Contents

Key to Route Maps

Each of the walks in this book is accompanied by a detailed map on which the route of the walk is shown in green. Places of interest along the walks – such as churches, pubs, houses and theatres where there have been reports of supernatural experiences – are clearly identified. Opening times are listed walk by walk at the back of the book, starting on page 148.

The following is a key to symbols and abbreviations used on the maps:

Symbols

route of walk

footpath

railway line

railway station

Underground station

major building

church

public toilets

site of haunting

site of murder

Abbreviations

APP	Approach	PDE	Parade
AVE	Avenue	PH	Public House
CLO	Close		(Pub)
COTTS	Cottages	PK	Park
CT	Court	PL	Place
DLR	Docklands	RD	Road
	Light	S	South
	Railway	SQ	Square
DRI	Drive	ST	Saint
E	East	ST	Street
GDNS	Gardens	STN	Station
GRN	Green	TER	Terrace
GRO	Grove	UPR	Upper
HO	House	VW	View
LA	Lane	W	West
LWR	Lower	WD	Wood
MS	Mews	WHF	Wharf
MT	Mount	WLK	Walk
N	North	WY	Way
PAS	Passage		

Introduction

London is steeped in history and legend and has the reputation of being the most haunted capital city in the world. The ghosts that occupy its streets and buildings provide fascinating glimpses of a brutal and gruesome past. The casual explorer, while visiting a church, a pub, a theatre or even an Underground station, may not suspect that there is a resident spook.

The aim of this book is to provide a series of atmospheric walks through London's haunted quarters. In the pages that follow you will find twenty-five walking tours covering different aspects or areas. The majority of the walks are in the London area, with the notable exception of Pluckley in Kent, which is a few hours' drive away and is acknowledged to be the most haunted village in England. Each tour has been paced out, to afford as much atmosphere as possible. I have avoided crowded streets, when there is a nearby, dark and sinister alternative. The walking tours include seven areas that are worth exploring even though the haunted sites do not present a suitable walking route. Rather than direct every step, I have described details of the ghostly activity and leave you to plan your own route using the accompanying maps. The final chapter, A Gaggle of Ghosts, features haunted places, with details of nearby Underground stations or other forms of transport.

I have tried to anticipate any questions, but I cannot answer the most obvious, which is whether you will see a ghost. Ghosts are tantalising and elusive. They are glimpsed for a fleeting moment and leave behind puzzled mortals. The majority of hauntings combine a feeling or instinct with an inexplicable coldness. You might smell or hear something, but you will rarely see anything. However, there are places that certainly do have a supernatural feeling and, if you are in the right place at the right time, you might just glimpse a ghostly presence and become one of the few who have walked with the dead.

So put on your walking shoes, put new batteries in the torch, wrap up warmly and set off into the darker recesses of haunted London. Good hunting.

Richard Jones
South Woodford

Map of London

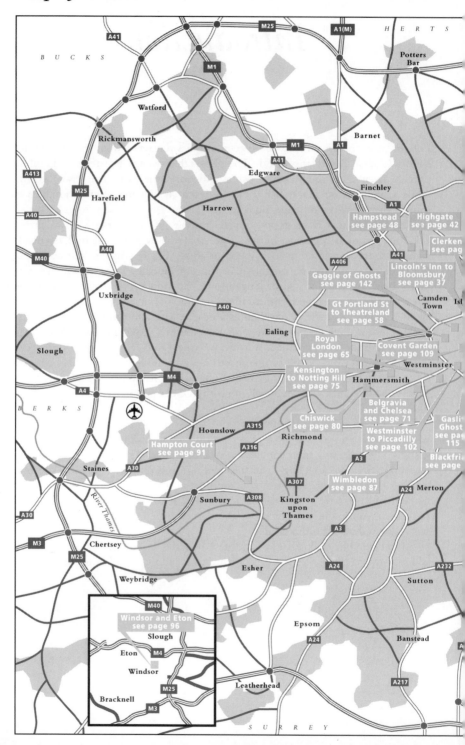

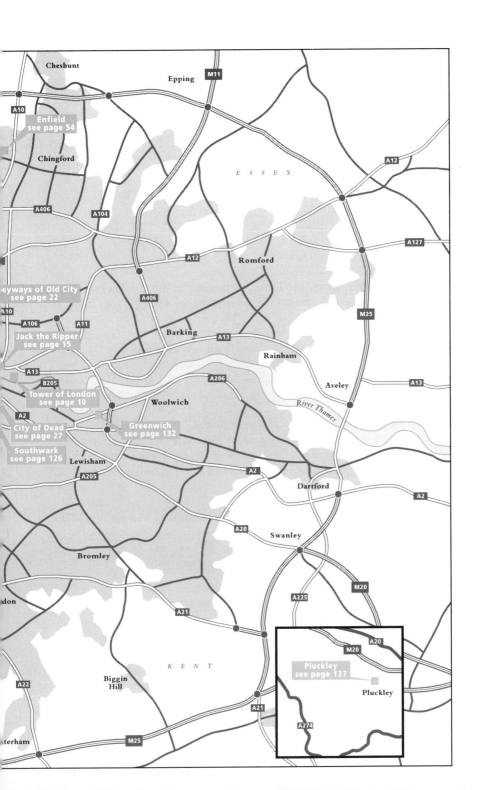

The Tower of London

Start/Finish	The Main Gate, Tower of London
Underground	Tower Hill Underground Station (Circle and District lines)
Duration	2 hours
Best Time	Later in the afternoon, when it's quieter
Refreshments	Various cafeterias around the Tower, or the Hung Drawn and Quartered public house

Grim, grey and awe-inspiring, the Tower has dominated the London landscape and the pages of history since its construction by William the Conqueror in 1078. Over the next five hundred years it evolved into a magnificent Royal Palace, home to successive monarchs. But it is its sinister reputation that brings the visitors flocking in their millions to hear tales of imprisonment, torture and execution. The names of those who passed through Traitor's Gate to be thereafter lost to the world read like a who's who of English history. Anne Boleyn, Lady Jane Grey, Guy Fawkes, Sir Walter Raleigh and many others spent their final days, months or even years incarcerated here. We can only guess at their suffering. Few left written accounts and often only the cold stone bore silent witness to their torment. So it comes as little surprise to discover that this building, with its gruesome and often tragic history, is the most haunted building in England, and its ghosts among the most illustrious.

Having cleared the security checks, pass beneath the Middle Tower (*c.*1280), where ghostly footsteps have been heard pacing backwards and forwards across the battlements. Continue to the Byward Tower (1280). In the 1980s a Yeoman Warder working here in the early hours of one morning looked up and was astonished to see two Beefeaters, dressed in the style of a much earlier period, standing on either side of the fireplace, smoking pipes and deep in conversation. As he stared at them, one of them suddenly turned, stared back and then both vanished.

St Thomas's Tower and an Invented Ghost

Walk through the Byward Tower, past the bookshop, and turn right up the stairs marked 'Medieval Palace and South Wall Walk'. These take you into the tower. In 1240 King Henry III ordered the construction of a watergate to fortify the Tower's riverside defences. Because it was built on marshland, setting the foundations was a difficult task and the edifice twice collapsed into the river. Noting that on each occasion this had happened on St George's Day, Henry asked the builders to account for the miraculous coincidence. Not wishing to admit incompetence, they invented a supernatural explanation – that, on both occasions, the ghost of Thomas à Becket had appeared and demolished the almost completed tower with his crosier.

Desperate to placate the spectral cleric, whose murder had been the result of the rash words of King Henry II, his own grandfather, Henry III ordered that a chapel dedicated to St Thomas must also be built. The structure was then completed without further ghostly interference, and has survived for nearly seven hundred years supported by little more than marshland and superstition.

The building has recently been opened to the public. It previously provided accommodation for the families of Tower officials, several of whom were troubled by the appearance of a ghostly monk whose sandals would be heard slapping on the stone floors. He occasionally shared his lonely vigil with the ghost of an unseen child whose heart-rending sobs were distressing for those who lived here.

Royal Murder in the Wakefield Tower

Pass through two rooms and you'll notice an eerie aura, with the feeling of isolation and coldness increasing as you turn left. Continue through a series of twisting staircases and arrive at the Wakefield Tower. That most tragic of monarchs, the unfortunate Henry VI, was imprisoned here. His weak and ineffectual reign ended with his imprisonment and murder before midnight on 21 May, 1471, as he knelt at the small window altar. It is believed, though not proven, that the dagger with which he was 'stikked full of deadly holes' was wielded by none other than the Duke of Gloucester (later the infamous Richard III). On the anniversary of his death, as the clock ticks towards midnight, Henry's pale and mournful wraith appears and paces fitfully around the room, until, as the last stroke of midnight chimes, he fades slowly into the stone and rests peacefully for another year.

The Salt Tower

Go through the door to the left of the altar (noting first the plaque commemorating the murder), up the winding staircase, and step from the shadows into daylight. Continue along the battlements (the views of the Thames and Tower Bridge to your right are spectacular), pass through the Lanthorn Tower, go down the stairs and turn right to reach the Salt Tower.

This grim building was once the Tower's darkest, dankest dungeon, used in the 16th century for the incarceration of Jesuit priests who bravely flouted the law of Henry VIII and continued to propagate the Catholic cause. Go up the stone staircase to the first floor, noting the huge and disproportionate fireplace. Note the graffiti chiselled into the bare walls by prisoners such as Henry Walpole, The Jesuit Priest, whose name can be seen in the alcove to the left of the fireplace. Imprisoned here in 1593, Walpole bravely resisted the horrendous torture inflicted upon him as the authorities attempted to extract the names of his Catholic contacts. But in the silent hours spent waiting for his next bout on the rack he prayed to the saints to give him courage, and carved their names on the wall, where they can still be seen today.

Some visitors, finding themselves alone here, have been surprised by a mysterious yellow glow that gets brighter and brighter and fills the room. They hear a low whispered murmuring like a voice at prayer, then suddenly feel the touch of ice-cold fingers on the back of the neck.

THE TOWER OF LONDON

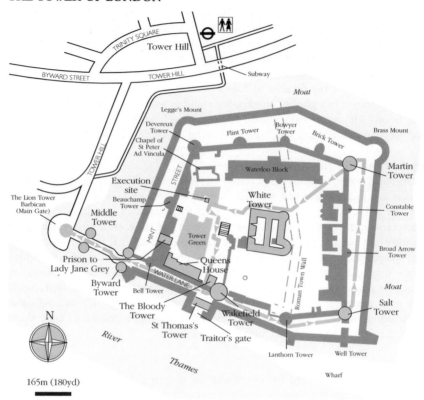

165m (180yd)

A Strange Appearance in the Martin Tower

Continue up the staircase and along the battlements, through the Broad Arrow and Constable towers. To your right, modern office and leisure complexes surround St Katharine's dock. Below you the traffic moves across Tower Bridge but, separated by the moat and high walls, you feel centuries removed from it. The walk brings you to the Martin Tower. One October night in 1817, the keeper of the Crown Jewels, Lenthal Swifte, had just sat down to dinner here, when his wife suddenly exclaimed, 'Good God! What is that?' A glass cylinder filled with a bluish-white fluid had appeared and was floating around the table. Swifte watched dumbstruck as it drifted behind his wife. 'Christ, it has seized me!' she screamed. Her terror moved the keeper to action and, leaping to his feet, he flung his chair at the apparition. It moved towards the window and vanished.

Ghosts of the White Tower

Leave the Martin Tower, taking extra care, since many visitors have complained of unseen hands pushing them as they descend the stairs. Go left and cross to the White Tower. This massive and forbidding tower is the oldest of the buildings and dwarfs others around it. Wandering through its massive galleries and winding stone corridors is eerie even during the day. At night, when the floorboards are settling and the shadows lengthening, it must take nerves of steel to walk alone inside the building. But the Custody Guards, whose job is to do just that, are a fearless bunch, although many of them have encountered strange phenomena.

A 'White Lady' who once stood at a window waving to a group of children and whose wraith now drifts silently around the rooms, is just one of its many spectres. Perhaps it is her cheap perfume that has been smelt around the entrance to St John's Chapel, causing many a Custody Guard to retch at its pungent aroma.

Guards passing from the chapel into the gallery containing Henry VIII's armour have spoken of a terrible crushing sensation that suddenly descends upon them, but which lifts the moment they stagger shaking from the room. One guard patrolling through here in the early hours of a stormy winter morning got a sudden and unnerving sensation that a black cloak had been flung over his head. As he struggled, the cloak was seized from behind by his phantom assailant and pulled tight around his throat. When he arrived at the guard room, after freeing himself, gasping and choking, the marks on his neck bore vivid testimony to his brush with the unseen horror. Another guard, Mr Arthur Crick, decided to rest for a moment one night as he made his rounds. Sitting on a ledge he slipped off his right shoe when a voice behind him whispered, 'There's only you and I here,' eliciting from Arthur the very earthly response, 'Just let me get this bloody shoe on and there'll be only you.'

Margaret Pole

Leave the White Tower and walk left to the grassy area lined with huge plane trees and patrolled by sinister-looking ravens. There is an old prophecy that, if the ravens leave the Tower, the monarchy will fall. These proud territorial birds are protected by royal decree, and the future of the monarchy is assured by the clipping of the ravens' wings. Go to the plaque marking the site of the scaffold and stand upon the spot where numerous illustrious people ended their days on the headsman's block. Many are buried in the church you are facing – St Peter Ad Vicula.

One execution, however, stands out as more shameful and gruesome than all the others, that of seventy-two-year-old Margaret Pole, Countess of Salisbury. Her crime was that she was the mother of Cardinal Pole, who from his safe haven in France had vilified Henry VIII's claim as head of the Church in England. Unable to punish the Cardinal, Henry opted to exact savage retribution by sentencing his mother to death. On 27 May, 1541, she stepped onto the scaffold and stared contemptuously at the executioner. When told to place her head on the block she refused. 'So should traitors do and I am none.' The executioner raised his axe, took a swing at her, then chased the screaming countess around the scaffold and hacked her to death. Her last moments have been played out on the anniversary of the shameful event ever since, as her screaming phantom attempts to escape from a ghostly executioner.

Lady Jane Grey

With your back to the block, walk along the pathway to the left of the lawn, pause by the final plane tree and look across to the dark brick house with the blue front door. Here another tragic resident, Lady Jane Grey, 'The Nine Day Queen', was kept prisoner. On 12 February, 1554, she watched from an upstairs window as her husband, Guildford Dudley, was led, sobbing, to his execution. Later that day, the sixteen-year-old girl, who had been pushed onto the throne by an ambitious father-in-law, walked bravely to her own death. Ever since, her ghost has appeared on the anniversary of her execution as a white shimmering figure that floats from the rolling river mists, strolls sadly around the green or glides along the battlements, then withers slowly away.

Anne Boleyn

The black-and-white timbered building to the left, known as the Queen's House, dates from 1530 and is the lodging of the Governor of the Tower of London. It was here that Anne Boleyn spent the days prior to her execution on 19 May, 1536, and it is here that her wraith returns – often with alarming consequences.

In 1864 a sentry was astonished by a headless figure, dressed in white, that suddenly came at him from the darkness. When his challenge failed to halt the spectre's advance, he raised his bayonet and charged. The weapon went straight through the figure and the sentry fainted from sheer terror. Found by his commanding officer, he was court-martialled for dereliction of duty, but was saved from disciplinary action by two witnesses who testified that they had seen the entire episode.

The Bloody Tower

Continue past the lawn and go straight into the Bloody Tower. The exhibition in the tower commemorates the imprisonment of Sir Walter Raleigh, and his ghost has been seen here on more than one occasion. But it is the little princes, Richard and Edward, whose tragic tale has given the Bloody Tower its sinister reputation. The boys were sent to the tower by their uncle Richard, Duke of Gloucester, in 1483 when he became Richard III, both boys mysteriously disappeared. It was always assumed that they had been murdered on Richard's instructions and their bodies buried somewhere within the grim fortress. When two skeletons were uncovered beneath a staircase of the White Tower in 1674 they were presumed to be the remains of the little princes and afforded royal burial in Westminster Abbey. But their whimpering ghosts, wearing white nightgowns and clutching each other in terror, often return to the dim rooms of their imprisonment. Witnesses are moved to pity, longing to reach out and console the spectral boys. But, if they do, the trembling wraiths back slowly towards the wall and fade into the fabric.

Leave the Bloody Tower and descend the staircase marked 'Exit'. Turn right, go under the Bloody Tower and you will see Traitor's Gate opposite. Kings, queens, lords, ladies, clerics and commoners would have taken their last look at the outside world from the top of those steps. The tower has been no respecter of birthright or rank. So offer a prayer for their repose as you shake the dust of history from your shoes and leave this grim fortress to its memories and shadows.

On the Trail of Jack the Ripper

Start	Whitechapel Underground Station (District and Hammersmith & City lines)
Finish	Liverpool Street Station (Central, Hammersmith & City, Metropolitan and British Rail main line)
Distance	5 miles (8 kilometres)
Duration	2½ hours
Best Times	Evenings and weekends when much of the route is deserted.
Refreshments	Numerous Indian restaurants around Brick Lane. Various pubs and cafés are passed.

Note that there is much more information available on this fascinating though grisly subject, and many books have been and continue to be written offering the 'Final Solution'. One of the best and most comprehensive is *The Jack the Ripper A–Z* by Paul Begg, Martin Fido and Keith Skinner.

In the autumn of 1888 a series of gruesome murders brought widespread panic to the streets of London's East End and sent shockwaves reverberating through polite society. The murderer became known as Jack the Ripper, and today that name is recognised the world over, conjuring up vivid images of gaslit, cobbled streets, thick swirling fog and the shadow of a top-hatted monster stalking the back alleyways in search of his unsuspecting prey. That no one was ever brought to justice for the murders has created one of the world's best-known whodunnits and has led to many fascinating theories as to his identity.

This walk will take you to each of the murder sites and lead you past many buildings associated with the hunt for the Ripper. You will journey along some very unsavoury and sinister old streets as you follow his bloodstained trail of terror through the districts of Spitalfields and Whitechapel.

Leave Whitechapel Underground Station, go right along Whitechapel Road and, a little way past the Grave Maurice pub, turn right into the narrow, arched and creepily sinister passageway called Wood's Buildings. Upon arrival at the massive building, which was formerly a school, walk counter-clockwise around it to Durward Street, go past the school and walk to the end of the long wall that lines the right side. It was here, at approximately 3.40am on 31 August, 1888 that a carter named Charles Cross spotted a heap lying in a gateway of what was then Buck's Row. Thinking it was a tarpaulin that might prove useful, he went to examine it and found the body of a woman, her skirt pulled up around her waist.

ON THE TRAIL OF JACK THE RIPPER

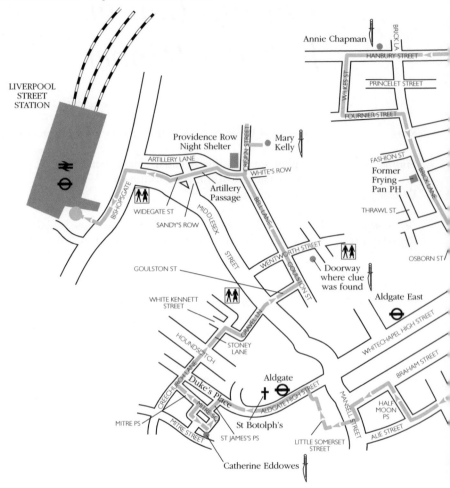

The Horror Begins

Within moments another carter, Robert Paul, arrived on the scene and the two raced off to find a policeman. They returned with three, one of whom, Constable Neil, shone his lantern onto the body and discovered that the throat had been cut back to the spine. The Jack the Ripper scare had begun. The woman was Mary Ann Nicholls, a forty-three-year-old prostitute, who had been thrown out of her lodging house two hours before because she did not have the money to pay her rent. 'I'll soon get my doss money,' she confidently predicted. 'See what a jolly bonnet I've got…' That bonnet now lay trampled and bloodstained in a Whitechapel gateway. What nobody noticed until later that day was that, beneath her blood-drenched clothing, a deep gash ran down her abdomen – she had been disembowelled.

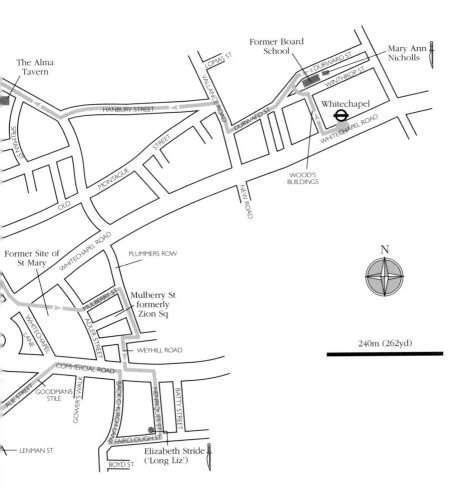

Residents of Buck's Row were not pleased with their sudden notoriety. A postman who took a ghoulish delight in going from house to house saying, for instance, 'Number 8 Murder Row, I believe,' led them to petition for a name change and, before the end of the year, the street had become Durward Street.

The Alma Tavern
Backtrack past the school building and go along Durward Street. Turn right into Vallance Road, cross the pedestrian crossing and go into the narrow alleyway marked Hanbury Street. A long walk now follows through an unremarkable postwar council estate. The building at the junction with Spelman Street was formerly the Alma Tavern. Named for the only Allied victory of the Crimean War, this pub was opened in 1854 by a returned soldier, Ed Tilney. By 1888 it had become one

of the area's notorious beer shops, where prostitutes and their clients would come to meet.

Continue along Hanbury Street – the smell of curry from the Indian restaurants that line your way hangs heavy and appetizingly in the air. Cross over Brick Lane and pause on the right about halfway along Hanbury Street by the wall of the Truman Brewery.

The Ripper Strikes Again

In the week that followed the murder of Mary Ann Nicholls, the newspapers carried sensational stories. They had wrongly ascribed the murders of Emma Smith on 3 April, 1888, and Martha Tabram or Turner on 6 August, 1888, to the Whitechapel Murderer. A possible suspect was 'Leather Apron', a man whom the prostitiutes claimed had made frequent threats to "rip them up". Unfortunately they did not know his name or address and the only description they could give was that he habitually wore a leather apron (the standard garment of Jewish butchers, carpenters and shoemakers) and sometimes a deerstalker cap. Just such a man was seen at 5.30am on 8 September, 1888, talking to a prostitute, Annie Chapman, in Hanbury Street. A little before 6am John Davis went into the back yard of number 29, found her mutilated body and went for the police. Her throat had been slashed twice and her intestines lay sprawled over her shoulder. Her murderer had slipped unnoticed into a busy street.

The left side of Hanbury Street is still much the same. The side where the murder occurred is now occupied by unappealing modern buildings that were formerly the headquarters of the Truman Brewery. The boardroom is said to strike deathly cold to the psychically inclined and the ghost of Annie Chapman is believed to walk there on the anniversary of her death.

The press now latched onto the 'Leather Apron' theory, noting that such a garment was found in the yard near the body. Lurid stories of a murderous immigrant incited mobs to attack innocent Jews. With the East End teetering on the brink of full-scale race rioting, police flooded into the streets and the investigation intensified.

Continue along Hanbury Street, go left into Wilkes Street and left into Fournier Street. Lined with delightful 18th-century buildings, which were built for Huguenot weavers, the street is still much as it was in 1888. Go right onto Brick Lane, to the junction with Thrawl Street, where an Indian restaurant now occupies what was formerly the Frying Pan public house (notice the name and crossed frying pans in brick relief on the upper gable). Mary Nicholls was seen wandering unsteadily from the pub at 2am on the morning of her murder. She boasted that she had already earned her "doss money" three times over but had drunk it away. Continue along Brick Lane, which becomes Osborne Street. At the traffic lights cross over Whitechapel Road and follow the right path through the green park. This was the site of St Mary's Church, destroyed in World War II. It was the medieval custom of lime-washing the exteriors of important buildings such as this that created the White Chapel which gave its name to the entire district.

Leave the park, go right into Adler Street, then left into Mulberry Street (known as Zion Square in 1888 and home to Aaron Kosminski, considered by many Ripperologists to be the likeliest of all the suspects). Turn right into Plumber's Row.

A Suspect is Found

On 10 September Sergeant William Thick arrived at 22 Mulberry Street and arrested thirty-six-year-old John Pizer, maintaining that he was 'Leather Apron'. However, Pizer had alibis for the nights of both murders and was eliminated from the inquiry.

At the end of Plumber's Row, turn right into Coke Street, first left into Weyhill Road, left onto Commercial Road, go over the pedestrian crossing and bear left then first right into Henrique Street, formerly Berners Street.

In 1888, at the junction with Fairclough Street, on the right, stood the International Workingmen's Educational Club. At 1am on 30 September, the club steward, Louise Diemschutz, drove his pony and cart into the yard. The animal shied and pulled to the right. Climbing down to investigate, Diemshutz noticed a woman lying behind the gates and presumed it was his wife and that she was drunk. However, his wife was elsewhere, perfectly sober, and he discovered that the woman had a gaping slash across her throat. Her name was 'Long Liz' Stride, and the fact that she had not been mutilated led the police to conclude that the arrival of the carriage had disturbed the murderer.

St Botolph's, Aldgate

Turn right along Fairclough Street, right onto Back Church Lane, left onto Commercial Road and, upon arrival at the Castle pub, go left down Goodman's Stile. Keep ahead into Aile Street, follow it over Leman Street at the traffic lights then, just after the White Swan pub, go right into Half Moon Passage. Go left onto Braham Street, cross Mansell Street at the pedestrian crossing, go left and first right into Little Somerset Street, and at its conclusion turn left onto Aldgate High Street. Go just past the Underground station, and on the right is the Church of St Botolph.

In 1888 the police offered prostitutes immunity from arrest if they confined their soliciting to the island on which the church stood. Nearby, at around 8.30pm on 29 September, a policeman arrested a local prostitute, Catherine Eddowes, for being drunk and took her to Bishopsgate Police Station, where she sobered up at around midnight, being then released at 1am. She walked out into the shadows and into the arms of the Ripper.

Murder in Mitre Square

Continue to the traffic lights, follow the two crossings right into Dukes Place (where at 1.35am Catherine was seen chatting amiably with a man, her hand on his chest) and, immediately after the school, go left into St James's Passage which leads into the square. Cross to the raised flowerbed and pause on the cobblestones, all that now remain of the original square. At 1.45am, P.C. Watkins found Catherine's body in the square. Her throat had been cut and her abdomen ripped open and savagely mutilated. V-shaped incisions had been made in her cheeks. Her eyes had been nicked through, the tip of her nose had been sliced off and her uterus and left kidney were missing.

The square has been completely transformed since that night – modern office blocks have sprung up where once stood grimy old warehouses. But those who pass this way in the early hours of the morning have occasionally glimpsed the spectral shape of the unfortunate victim, lying upon the spot where her life came to such a gruesome end.

It was after this night that the murderer was given his nickname. A letter that had been posted to the Central News Agency and purported to come from the killer was released; it bore the chilling signature 'Jack the Ripper'. It was certainly a hoax, and probably the work of a journalist, but the name gripped the public imagination and created the world's first media murderer. The Ripper did leave behind a clue, and as a result we know exactly where he went from here. To follow in his footsteps, stand with your back to the flower bed, go left across the square and through dark and gloomy Mitre Passage, then turn right onto Creechurch Lane.

The Clue

Cross over the pedestrian crossing, over Houndsditch and into Stoney Lane. Continue right into White Kennett Street, then go left into Gravel Lane, over Middlesex Street (site of the Petticoat Lane street market) and along New Goulston Street, and turn left into Goulston Street, where on the right, in the stairway after number 48, the clue was found. This massive building today provides luxury dwellings for City workers but in 1888 it was occupied mostly by Jews who traded secondhand clothes on nearby Petticoat Lane and sold shoes at the footwear market on Wentworth Street.

At 2.50am P.C. Alfred Long found in the doorway, a piece of Catherine Eddowes's shabby apron, sticky with blood. It seemed that the Ripper had used it to wipe his hands and the blade of his knife. This tells us where the Ripper was heading, and confirms the theory that he was an East Ender, living in the area.

Dorset Street

Continue over Wentworth Street, go along Bell Lane to Crispin Street and, after the multi-storey car park, turn right into a now unnamed private road which in 1888 was Dorset Street. In a long-vanished passage called Miller's Court lived Mary Kelly, a vivacious twenty-five-year-old Irish girl. Between 3.30 and 4.00am on 9 November neighbours heard a woman's voice that may have been Mary's cry out, 'MURDER!' The cry was ignored by all who heard it. Later that day her landlord's agent called to collect her overdue rent. He looked through a broken windowpane and saw a sight that sent him reeling back in horror. Mary had been so horribly mutilated that her face was barely recognisable, and her virtually skinned carcass could hardly be described as a body.

The Ripper had struck again, but the bloodbath at Miller's Court would be his swansong. Despite several subsequent scares, the Ripper stepped from Mary Kelly's room and disappeared as suddenly and mysteriously as he had appeared twelve weeks before. The identity of the Ripper has never been discovered, and the suspects range from a grandson of Queen Victoria (the Duke of Clarence) to an American doctor.

In 1910 Sir Robert Anderson, who at the time of the killings had been Assistant Commissioner of the Metropolitan Police, wrote in his memoirs that the Ripper was a poor Polish Jew living in the neighbourhood. Chief Inspector Swanson, the man who headed the original investigation, pencilled onto the margin of those memoirs that the Ripper's name was Kosminski, whose house site you passed earlier in the walk.

A grim, fortress-like building stands on the other side of Crispin Street from the car park. It is the only building in the immediate vicinity to survive from that long-ago night when a lone cry of 'MURDER' and a shadow moving quickly through the darkness marked the end of the Ripper's reign of terror. Opened in 1860, it was formerly the Providence Row Night Shelter, where nuns attempted to ease the suffering of those unfortunates whom Victorian society chose to ignore.

Go along Artillery Lane to the left of the Shelter and straight ahead through the wonderfully atmospheric Artillery Passage. Cross Sandy's Row into Widegate Street, go ahead into Middlesex Street, cross Bishopsgate and turn left to arrive at Liverpool Street Station and the end of the walk.

Alleyways of the Old City

Start	Liverpool Street Station (Central, Circle, Hammersmith & City, Metropolitan and British Rail main line)
Finish	Mansion House Underground Station (Circle and District Lines)
Distance	2 miles (3.2 kilometres)
Duration	1½ hours
Best Times	The area is most atmospheric at weekends or weekday evenings. However, at these times you will not be able to visit any of the interiors listed.
Refreshments	The area is devoid of refreshment stops at week ends and in the evenings. At other times you can stop at Williamson's, Ye Old Watling and numerous sandwich bars.

The Eastern fringe is the oldest part of the City, with a labyrinth of historic alleyways that snake their way between towering office blocks where London's financial institutions occupy the wealthiest square mile on earth.

This walk delves into those shadowy passages and takes you along streets that have changed little in over a hundred years. It is an area that Dickens knew well, and he set many of his works around here, most notably using it as the location for Scrooge's counting house in *A Christmas Carol*. There are dusty old churches in abundance, 18th-century eating houses at which you can still dine, and an array of famous landmarks including the home of the Lord Mayor and the Bank of England, where the nation's gold reserves lie safe beneath a tranquil churchyard.

Leave Liverpool Street Station through the main line station via the Bishopsgate exit, and turn right. Cross over Liverpool Street itself and, just past the White Hart pub, go right into White Hart Court. Go left through the bollards, right along Alderman's Walk and left along an unnamed path, then turn left and walk to the Church of St Botolph's Without Bishopsgate.

One Saturday afternoon in 1982, photographer Chris Brackley took a photograph of the inside of this splendid church. On developing the picture he saw to his surprise the figure of a woman in old-fashioned garb standing on the right balcony. The only two people in the church when the photograph was taken were Chris and his wife. As there was no double exposure of the film, and his equipment was not faulty, it seemed that Chris had photographed a ghost.

The story took a bizarre twist a few years later when a builder contacted Chris and told him that, while working on the restoration of the crypt, he had knocked down a wall and accidentally disturbed a pile of dusty old coffins, one of which came open. Gazing back at him was a reasonably well preserved body whose face bore an uncanny resemblance to that of the woman in Chris's picture. The picture is reproduced as plate 4; I leave it to you to draw your own conclusions.

St Peter upon Cornhill

Leave the church and turn left and then right along Bishopsgate. Cross Wormwood Street and continue along an uninspiring section of the walk. It is well worth making a detour to the clearly signed St Helen's Church.

Cross Threadneedle Street and take the next right along Cornhill. A little way along on the left is the Church of St Peter upon Cornhill. Reputedly founded on the site of the Roman basilica by Lucius, the first Christian King of Britain in AD179, the church appears curious, dwarfed by surrounding developments.

The red terracotta building to the right of the church is surmounted by two ferocious-looking demons, who crouch as though ready to leap from their perches and wreak mayhem in the church. They represent the culmination of a bitter feud that erupted between the vicar of St Peter's and the architect of this building, a Mr Rentz. The original plans meant his new building would have encroached on land owned by the church, and the vicar caused such a furore that the architect had to redesign the building at great cost of both time and money. Rentz added the grotesques as a curse upon the little church and, it is said, modelled the face of the fiercest demon on that of his arch enemy, the vicar of St Peter's.

Walk along Cornhill, and upon arrival at the Church of St Michael go left into St Michael's Alley. In the window of the Jamaica Wine House you can see ledgers with records of long-ago transactions. The alleyway is darkly sinister; even the London traffic and everyday bustle are strangely muffled. It was here that Charles Dickens placed the office of Ebenezer Scrooge. The neighbourhood has changed much since, but here in this backwater of grimy alleyways time stands still, and you can picture its Victorian residents going 'wheezing up and down, beating their hands on their breasts, and stamping their feet upon the pavement stones to warm them'.

Further along the alley you arrive at a truly Dickensian landmark, the George and Vulture, a traditional city chop-house where, for almost three hundred years City bankers, financiers and stockbrokers have enjoyed their ale and mutton chops. Today the rooms upstairs are visited occasionally by a Victorian lady in a long grey dress who floats silently around rooms and drifts along corridors.

Turn right just before the George and Vulture, then right again into Ball Court, a deliciously dark and gloomy alleyway that twists under and between several old buildings before emerging back onto Cornhill.

The Bank of England and 'The Old Lady in Black'

Turn left, go over the crossing, continue left and then turn first right into Royal Exchange Buildings. Upon arrival at the statue of George Peabody (founder in the 19th century of the Peabody Trust, which still provides quality low-cost housing to London's less well off), go left over Threadneedle Street and, keeping ahead over Bartholomew Lane, pause upon arrival at the huge doors through which can be glimpsed Garden Court at the Bank of England. Secure and unwelcoming as these windowless, 18th-century walls appear, it comes as a pleasant surprise to find that at the centre of this fortress, where the nation's gold reserves are kept, there stands not a vast impenetrable vault but a tranquil garden that once belonged to the Church of St Christopher le Stocks, demolished when the bank was extended in 1781.

The bank's most persistent ghost is that of Sarah Whitehead, whose brother Philip was executed for forgery in 1812. Refusing to accept both his guilt and his death, Sarah would call daily at the bank to ask the staff if they had seen her brother. They humoured her at first and would reply that Philip had not been in that day, promising to tell him she was inquiring after him. She would nod, smile and shuffle out into the street. The black crepe dress she wore earned her the nickname 'The Bank Nun'. By 1818 the bank's governors grew tired of her daily visits and gave her a sum of money on condition she agreed never to return to the bank. In life she kept that contract, but after her death, her wraith has often broken it. More than one late-night reveller, wending a weary way home along Threadneedle Street, has been surprised by 'The Old Lady in Black' who appears from nowhere and with downcast eyes, inquires sadly but politely: 'Have you seen my brother?'

Continue along Threadneedle Street, cross Prince's Street and follow the path as it bends left and then right. You will pass several entrances to Bank Underground Station. A dreadful smell, 'like an open grave', and a feeling of melancholic desolation are said to hang in the air and disturb late-night maintenance workers at this station. It is thought it could be connected with the proximity to Liverpool Street Station, said to have been built on the site of a plague pit.

The Curse of St Mary le Bow

Move swiftly into Poultry and keep ahead into Cheapside. Clearly visible on the left is the Church of St Mary le Bow. Go to the right of the tower into Bow Churchyard and descend the stone steps at the southwest corner of the church. These lead to an atmospheric crypt whose walls date from the 9th and 10th centuries. Here you can see the bows or arches that give the church its name. In the 11th and 12th centuries black masses were held at the church during the hours of darkness, and requiem masses for the living were also held.

A series of tragedies struck the neighbourhood and it became common knowledge that St Mary Le Bow was cursed. The roof blew off in 1090, resulting in considerable loss of life. In 1196 William Fitzosbert (known as Long Beard) killed one of the Archbishop of Canterbury's soldiers who had been sent to arrest him (his crime was to preach against excessive taxation), and took sanctuary in the church tower. The building was almost destroyed as he was being smoked out. In 1271 the tower toppled into the street, killing more people, and, once it had been rebuilt, Lawrence Duckett was murdered there, in reprisal for which seventeen men were hanged and a woman burnt. It was rebuilt several times after being destroyed by the Great Fire and much later the bombs of the Blitz, but has since enjoyed a period of relative good fortune. The authorities feel so confident that the curse has been lifted that a health-food restaurant now occupies one section of the crypt.

Go back up the stairs, turn left from the gates and follow Bow Churchyard, then turn right into Bow Lane.

ALLEYWAYS OF THE OLD CITY

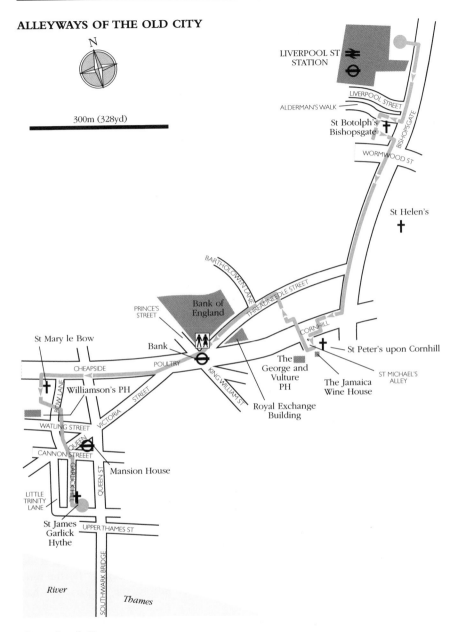

Groveland Court

This pedestrian thoroughfare is a delightful throwback to bygone London, lost in a jungle of modern city buildings. A little way along turn right into Groveland Court. One evening a policeman was surprised when his highly trained, fearless police dog whimpered and growled, and adamantly refused to go into the court. In the late 1930s, a similar feeling caused another police officer to 'stumble as if he had been pushed from behind and crack his head upon the paving stones'.

Entering Grovelands Court you find Williamson's Tavern, a delightful hostelry that stands at the exact centre of the City of London. Reputed to stand on the site of the home of Sir John Oldcastle, the model for Shakespeare's Falstaff, the building became the home of successive Lord Mayors before being turned into an hotel by the Williamson family in the 18th century. In the 1930s the pub was rebuilt by Mr William Hollis Jr, a surveyor, who found himself troubled by ghostly activity. Queer noises were heard on Saturday nights, and a ghostly form was frequently seen gliding over Groveland Court. The disturbances proved too much for Mr Hollis who decided to 'leave the ghost to its own devices... and the estate is now on the market.'

St James Garlick Hythe

Return to Bow Lane and turn right. Go ahead over Watling Street and pass Ye Olde Watling Pub, by the architect Sir Christopher Wren whose building was originally erected to house his workmen. Cross the pedestrian crossings over Queen Victoria Street and Cannon Street. To the side of Mansion House Underground Station, descend Garlick Hill to reach the Church of St James Garlick Hythe. In 1855 workmen clearing out the vicar's vault at this particularly exquisite Wren church uncovered the corpse of a man who became known to generations of parishioners as 'Jimmy Garlick'. For many years he was kept in a glass case inside the church, and beneath him was placed the salutary message:

> *Stop Stranger Stop As You Pass By.*
> *As You Are Now So Once Was I.*
> *As I Am Now So Shall You Be.*
> *So Pray Prepare To Follow Me.*

Impish choirboys used to take him out on Sundays and sit him in a pew with a ruff collar around his neck. During the Blitz, a bomb came uncomfortably close to his cabinet, shattering glass over his mummified corpse.

Ever since, the ghost of Jimmy Garlick has haunted the church. Later in the War a fire-watcher spotted a dark figure walking along an aisle during an air raid and shouted at it to take cover, whereupon the ghost just faded away before his eyes. In the 1970s an American tourist visited the church with her two sons, and the elder of the two went off exploring. Climbing the stairs to the balcony, he came face-to-face with a skeletal figure, its hands crossed over its chest. It said nothing but stood staring at the terrified boy, its white eyes bulging from bony sockets. By the time the boy was able to attract his mother's attention the apparition had disappeared.

Jimmy now resides in an upper room in the tower of the church, though plans have been mooted to place him again on public display. It is now thought he was sixteen year-old Seagrave Chamberlain, who died from a fever on 17 December, 1765. His wall monument can be found at the west end of the north aisle.

Leave the church and go back to the top of Garlick Hill to reach Mansion House Underground Station and the end of the walk.

The City of the Dead

Start	St Paul's Underground Station (Central Line)
Finish	Barbican underground station (Circle, Hammersmith & City, Metropolitan lines and British Rail)
Distance	1½ miles (2.4 Kilometres)
Duration	1 hour 20 minutes
Best Times	Most atmospheric at weekends. St Bartholomew's Church closes at 4pm.
Refreshments	The Viaduct Tavern and the Rising Sun (both covered on the walk) plus numerous cafés in Smithfield Market.

If there is any truth in the theory that buildings record the events that happen within them and that walls are charged with the energy, personalities and emotions of those who have lived there, then this area has nigh on two thousand years and millions of events crackling within its ancient fabric. For it is an area where a 16th-century gatehouse stands cheek by jowl alongside a magnificent Norman church, and a cherubic fat boy marks the spot where the Great Fire ended in 1666. It is where the Romans built sturdy walls to protect their city of Londinium and where much later, magnificent medieval monasteries flourished. London's grimmest prison stood here and citizens flocked in their thousands to enjoy the macabre spectacle of public executions.

Leave St Paul's Underground Station by the cathedral exit and turn left onto Newgate Street. Cross at the crossings and enter the small alleyway to the left of the ruined church (destroyed by World War II bombing).

Greyfriars Passage and Two Murderous Wives

This is the site of an ancient burial ground where lie the mortal remains of 'the she-wolf of France', Queen Isabella, wife of the English King Edward II. With her lover, Roger Mortimer, she instigated the deposing of the king and had him imprisoned at Berkeley Castle. On the night of 21 September, 1327, he was brutally murdered by way of 'a kind of horn or funnel... thrust into his fundament through which a red hot spit was run up his bowels'. His screams could be heard far outside the castle walls, and are still heard there on the anniversary of the horrific event. Following Mortimer's execution by her the king's son, Edward III, in 1330, Isabella retreated into a polite retirement. She died in 1358, her last years having been racked by violent dementia. She was buried here at Greyfriars, with the heart of Edward II placed upon her breast. At twilight, her beautiful, angry ghost flits amongst the trees and bushes, clutching the beating heart of her murdered husband before her.

THE CITY OF THE DEAD

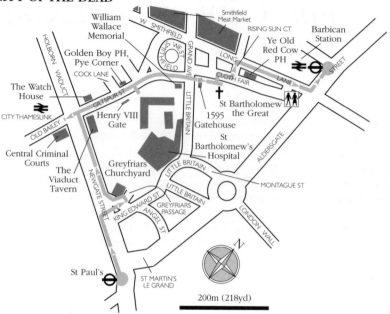

Lady Alice Hungerford was considered a great beauty of the Tudor age and she too murdered her spouse, in her case with a lethal dose of poison. In 1523 she paid for her crime by being boiled alive. She was laid to rest at Greyfriars, where her beautiful, serene phantom was soon drifting through the cloisters and aisles of the monastery and, following its dissolution, through the burial ground that sprang up on its site.

And so the two ladies went about their nocturnal rambles, each blissfully unaware of the other's existence, until one night, in Victorian times, they met among the tombs. Eyeing each other with curiosity, then surprise and finally hostility, they each became jealous of the other's beauty, and a fearsome battle erupted as they fought over their territory. Bemused witnesses could only look on in terror as the spectral fight became more and more vicious. A night watchman, caught up in the midst of the ghostly squabbling, was so frightened by the experience that he fled the scene and 'never … came back to collect his pay'.

Leave the peaceful churchyard, then go back to and turn right along Newgate Street. Characterless 19th-century developments now line a thoroughfare where butchers once plied their trade and which was known accordingly as Blow Bladder Lane.

Witchcraft at the Central Criminal Courts

Upon arrival at the junction with Giltspur Street cross to the courts, better known, the world over, by the name of the street in which they stand – Old Bailey. This was the site of Newgate Prison and public executions were carried out in the square outside from 1783 until their abolition in 1868, with as many as 20,000 people cramming into the area to ensure themselves a good view. The prison was demolished in the early 1900s and the courts were built on the site. They are open to the public, who can attend the trials.

It might come as a surprise to learn that the last witchcraft trial in England was held at the Old Bailey as recently as March 1944. The unfortunate witch was the Scottish medium, Mrs Helen Duncan. The specific charge against her was pretending 'to raise the spirits of the dead'. The case so annoyed Winston Churchill that he fired off an angry missive to the Home Secretary demanding to know why the 1735 Witchcraft Act was 'being used in a modern court of justice'. The defence even offered to hold a seance in the courtroom and allow the spirits to testify on Mrs Duncan's behalf, but the jury, disappointingly, declined. The unfortunate medium was found guilty and spent nine months in Holloway Prison. Her supporters maintain that her trial and imprisonment were due to official paranoia and that the government actually feared she might 'see' and reveal the preparations for the D-Day landings. As a direct result of the trial, the Witchcraft Act was repealed in 1951 and replaced by the Fraudulent Medium's Act.

The Poltergeist of the Viaduct Tavern

This pub is on the corner opposite the courts. It dates from 1875 and is the last example of a late Victorian gin palace left in the City of London. It is also prone to poltergeist activity. "Poltergeist" comes from the German terms *Poltern* "to knock" and *Geist* "spirit" but is now generically applied to any noisy ghost. This one is renowned for taking customer's drinks when they are not looking, and for switching the lights off in the ladies' toilet. Much of the phenomenon emanates from the cellars, which you can visit with a member of staff. Descend a rickety flight of creaking wooden stairs and note the sudden drop in temperature. Two heavy, wooden doors lead to an inner section that smells musty and damp. Circling it are five brick cavities, set back from the main cellar. Stand in the far cavity on the right (where several mediums have sensed something) and notice a feeling of melancholy. The light here is dim, and shadows creep up the walls and spread out across the ceilings. Many bar staff refuse to work down here alone and those who do have suffered the unwelcome attentions of 'Fred'.

A manager, tidying the end room one Saturday morning, was suddenly plunged into darkness when all the lights went out. Feeling his way to the door, he found to his dismay that it would not open. Fortunately, his wife heard his screams, and found that the doors, which would not open from the inside, were unlocked and easily pushed open from the outside.

The Golden Boy of Pye Corner

Leave the pub and walk right along Giltspur Street. Note the watchhouse on the left, built in 1761, where a night watchman would guard the churchyard behind from the activities of the bodysnatchers. Cross over to Cock Lane, next left, and look up at the Golden Boy on the wall. He marks the spot where the Great Fire burnt itself out in 1666. The fact that the fire began in Pudding Lane and finished here at Pye Corner was seen by Londoners as a clear sign from God, that the conflagration was punishment for their overindulgence, hence the information beneath the Golden Boy himself:

This boy is in memory put up for the Late Fire of London
Occasion'd by the Sin of Gluttony 1666

In 1762 Cock Lane was visited by thousands of people hoping to hear the scratching of the infamous ghost that was making nightly contact at number 33. The full story is covered on page 34.

Weird Tales of St Bartholomew's Hospital and Smithfield

Cross left over Giltspur Street and continue to the main gate of the hospital. Above the gate of the hospital is the only statue of Henry VIII in London. The gate itself was built in 1702 by the stonemasons working on St Paul's Cathedral.

In the depths of this, London's oldest hospital, is the 'Coffin Lift'. In the silent hours of early mornings, it has been known to take bemused passengers down to the basement, irrespective of the floor they have requested. The story is that a nurse was once murdered in the elevator, and that it is her spirit that causes the malfunction, leaving staff stranded at the lower levels of the hospital. Many who then use the stairs find to their horror that the lift begins to move up the well around which the stairs twist following their progress from level to level.

The hospital is also haunted by the 'Grey Lady' of Grace Ward, said to be the ghost of a nurse who administered a fatal overdose to a patient and, in her remorse, committed suicide. Nurses have experienced feeling a light tap on their shoulder, and suddenly becoming aware of her presence as she stands, shaking her head in warning.

Continue along Giltspur Street. The wall on your right still bears shrapnel damage from a Zeppelin raid in 1916. Pause on the right at the Memorial to Sir William Wallace. In August 1305 Sir William was executed here on what was then the Smoothfield, now Smithfield. This wide open space was used for public executions, and many unfortunate souls suffered a variety of gruesome deaths that included boiling and roasting alive.

In the reign of Queen Mary Tudor over two hundred Protestants were put to death, many being burnt here at Smithfield. 'Bloody Mary' insisted that green wood should not be used, since it smoked and its victims were likely to suffocate before suffering the full agony of the flames. Today, black cabs park where the stake once stood, and lorries arrive from all over Europe, offloading animal carcasses for Smithfield Meat Market, opposite. But those who work in the area say that sometimes, early on misty mornings, the smell of burning flesh drifts across the square and agonised screams rend the air.

The black-and-white timber building ahead dates from 1595 and, as you pass through the gateway beneath, the mood changes immediately. An uneven flagstone path goes by a churchyard that rises some six feet into the air. This elevation is caused by the number of people buried, one on top of the other, on the other side of the wall.

Priory Church of St Bartholomew the Great

Ahead of you, London's oldest parish church is overhung by huge trees, whose gnarled branches reach across and scratch lightly against its dark, flintstone exterior. The pathway slopes downward and arrives at the entrance to the church, which was founded in 1123 by a monk named Rahere, who reputedly began his career as jester to the Court of King Henry I. Walk into an interior where little has changed in hundreds of years. The air is heavy and musty, and even on a bright summer's day the church is dimly lit. Beneath your feet, in dusty vaults that have seen no daylight for a hundred and more years, those who worshipped here in the 17th, 18th and early 19th centuries lie interred. Occasionally the silence is shattered by an unseen organist, whose tuneful wailing bounces from the walls, rebounds along the aisles and fades into the gloomy shadows of the church's hidden recesses. Massive stone pillars and graceful arches span walls that literally drip with atmosphere.

To the left of the altar is the tomb of the church's founder, Rahere. The stonework at the rear shows the result of a hasty repair, carried out in the 19th century when the authorities decided to report upon the state of the founder's body. It was well preserved, and even the clothes and sandals were still intact. Two days later one of the officers of the church fell ill and confessed that, when the tomb had been open, he had stolen a sandal. He gave it back and recovered, but it was never returned to the foot of its rightful owner, and since that day Rahere has haunted the church as a shadowy, cowled figure who appears from the gloom, brushes by astonished witnesses and fades slowly into thin air.

On other occasions his appearances have been more active. Earlier this century, the Reverend W.F.G. Sandwich was showing two ladies around the church when he sighted a monk standing in the pulpit, giving a very animated sermon to an unseen congregation – although no sound could be heard. The two ladies apparently could see nothing, but just to be sure he directed their attention to the pulpit, making the observation, 'I don't think that pulpit is worthy of the church, do you?' The ladies merely agreed, obviously quite unaware of the ghostly monk.

Ye Old Red Cow

Leave the church, go up the steps to the right and walk through the churchyard. Cross Cloth Fair, go through Rising Sun Court to the left of the Rising Sun pub, and turn right along Long Lane to arrive at Ye Old Red Cow.

This pub was for many years, under the tenancy of Dick O'Shea a characterful Irishman who attracted the likes of Bernard Miles and Peter Ustinov to try his legendary hot whisky toddies. The pub was open from 6.30am, serving the workers after their evening duties at Smithfield Market, opposite. Dick would sit in his rocking chair on the upper balcony keeping a patronly eye on his customers below. He died in 1981 but, for almost a year afterwards, regulars often caught sight of him, sitting on the balcony, rocking back and forth, as genial and watchful a host in death as he had been in life. The pub unfortunately has now been radically altered so the balcony is sadly no more.

Continue along Long Lane to the traffic lights and turn left to arrive at Barbican Underground Station and the end of the walk.

Clerkenwell

Start	Barbican Underground Station (Circle, Hammersmith & City, Metropolitan Lines and British Rail)
Finish	Farringdon Underground Station (same lines as Barbican)
Distance	2 miles (3.2 kilometres)
Duration	1½ hours
Best Times	Weekends, when the streets are relatively deserted.
Refreshments	Several pubs and sandwich bars are scattered around the area, but most are closed at weekends.

This walk goes through a quirky little quarter of London that is perched on a hill overlooking the Fleet River valley. It is named for the well where parish clerks would gather on feast days and holidays. The area is richly furnished with historic remnants that have sinister and gruesome histories. These include an eerie plague pit, a delightful Tudor manor house, a splendid medieval gate, a grim underground prison and the crumbling remains of the well. The variety of its features is matched by the diversity of its ghosts. There are screaming children, ghostly monks, shadowy figures, an infamous 18th-century haunting and, for the first time in this book, a traditional nobleman carrying his head under his arm.

The Amorous Ghost of the Sutton Arms

Leave Barbican Underground Station and go left along Aldersgate Street and first left into Carthusian Street, where on the right is an enchanting bow-windowed pub, the Sutton Arms, haunted by a red-headed gentleman in old-fashioned dress, whom the manager has christened 'Charley'. In October 1997 a friend of the landlord was combing her hair when a cold chill suddenly passed over her. Looking in the mirror, she saw a red-haired man standing directly behind her but, on spinning round, she found she was alone in the room. Two girls enjoying a lunchtime drink in the main bar were not amused when 'Charley' appeared between them, grinned, and vanished as abruptly as he had appeared.

Continue along Carthusian Street, turn right into Charterhouse Square and stop by the railings that enclose the grassy area. Many people consider this to be one of the neighbourhood's most melancholic spots. The huge plane trees that tower above the peaceful lawns stand over a plague pit where 50,000 victims of the 1348 Black Death are said to be buried. Some of them would, no doubt, have been buried alive, and people walking by the square during the hours of darkness can sometimes hear the anguished screams of these poor unfortunates as they relive their final agonies amid the putrefying corpses. When the Charterhouse School stood nearby, new pupils were dared to creep into the square as midnight approached, press an ear to the cold earth and, as the witching hour chimed, listen to the screeching and howling that they were assured would sound from beneath the grass.

The Charterhouse Wraiths

Follow the railings counterclockwise around the square and stop when you arrive opposite the massive and ancient wooden gates of the Charterhouse. In 1381 Sir Walter de Manny endowed a monastery alongside the plague pit for the strict order of the Carthusians. The monastery flourished until the Reformation, when the monks refused to accept Henry VIII as head of the church. The Prior, John Houghton, was hanged, drawn and quartered, and one of his arms was nailed to the gates. During the next few weeks, as the surviving monks continued to hold out against the king's demands, they were visited by long-dead brethren who urged them to stay true to their faith. One dark wintry night, as the brothers prayed by dim candlelight, there was a flash of heavenly flame and every candle flared up with a celestial brilliance. This encouraged the Carthusians to stay true to their beliefs, even though sixteen more were executed before the monastery was dissolved and the surviving friars fled into exile.

The remains of the monastery were granted to Lord North, who turned it into a splendid private residence. He entertained Elizabeth I here on two occasions, his hospitality being so lavish that he crippled himself financially and had to retire to the country. The house was then bought by Thomas Howard, 4th Duke of Norfolk, whose plans to marry Mary Queen of Scots led to his execution in 1572. In 1611 it was purchased by the hugely wealthy Sir Thomas Sutton, who converted it into a hospital for aged men and a school for the education of the sons of the poor. In time it became a distinguished public school; and moved to new premises in Godalming in 1867. Today some twenty or so elderly men still live in this wonderful mansion, amid ancient courts and forgotten cloisters.

At night, when the streets fall silent, a shadowy monk is said to drift aimlessly about the cobblestoned courtyards, parts of which survive from the days of the monastery. He shares his weary vigil with the spectre of the Duke of Norfolk, who comes striding down the main staircase, head tucked neatly under his arm, as he returns to the spot where he was arrested.

Leave the square through the iron gates into Fox and Knot Street. Pass on the right the wonderfully Gothic frontage of the Fox and Anchor pub, from which hideous grotesques scowl down upon passers-by. Keep to the right pavement (the buildings opposite are those of Smithfield Meat Market, built in 1868) and turn right into St John's Street, where post-war architecture nestles cheek by jowl with sturdy pre-war dwellings, many of which have now metamorphosed into restaurants and theme bars. Three-quarters of the way along on the left the narrow Passing Alley squeezes itself between two high, dark brick walls and delivers you onto St John's Lane, where you will find yourself in disbelief at a medieval gate that spans the walkway and stands dwarfed by towering blocks of drab offices. This is St John's Gate, built in 1504 as the main entrance to the Priory of St John of Jerusalem. Here, in 1877, the St John Ambulance Brigade was founded.

The Cock Lane Ghost

Go through the gate and over Clerkenwell Road straight ahead into St John's Square. A little way along on the right, look through the gates where, to the left, can be seen the remains of St John's Clerkenwell. It was in a vault beneath this church that London's most famous haunting reached its inglorious finale.

In 1760 William Parsons offered lodgings to a widower called William Kent in his house in Cock Lane. Kent gratefully accepted and brought with him his sister-in-law, Miss Fanny, with whom he had become romantically involved. Parsons borrowed a considerable sum of money from his lodger and showed a determined reluctance to repay it. When Kent was called away on business his mistress, rather than sleep alone, took Parsons's eleven-year-old daughter, Elizabeth, to sleep in her bed. In the middle of the night they were woken by a mysterious scratching noise and Fanny convinced herself that it was the spirit of her dead sister, come to warn her of her own imminent demise. When Kent returned he found his lover on the verge of a nervous breakdown and decided it best that they move as soon as possible. No sooner had they done so than the unfortunate Fanny died of smallpox, to be buried in a vault at St John's Clerkenwell. The mysterious noises were heard again in Parsons's house. When Kent pressed Parsons to repay the borrowed money, he responded by claiming that the spirit of Miss Fanny was behind the haunting and that she had informed him that William Kent had murdered her. When news spread that a vengeful ghost was communicating through Elizabeth Parsons, Londoners flocked to the house in Cock Lane, where they listened as the revenant accused Kent of poisoning her with arsenic. Parsons did a roaring trade, charging an entrance fee to his house, and creating extra income for local shopkeepers.

But then a local clergyman announced that, since the spirit was apparently accusing William Kent of a serious crime, an investigation should be carried out by a group of eminent men. The ghost proved more than willing to oblige and announced, through Parsons, that if they would care to spend a night by Miss Fanny's resting place she would answer their questions by knocking on the lid of her coffin. And so it was that the great Dr Samuel Johnson led a group of fearless investigators down into the crypt at one o'clock one morning. However, when by dawn nothing had happened, Johnson declared the ghost a fraud.

A secret watch was kept on Elizabeth, who was observed hiding a small wooden board under her stays, and the trick was exposed. Parsons spent two years in the King's Bench Prison. Elizabeth was exonerated of any crime, it being decided that she was not a willing accomplice. Kent's name was cleared, London settled back into the Age of Reason and the ghost was assigned to the pages of history as 'Scratching Fanny of Cock Lane'. Continue across St John's Square, go through Jerusalem Passage, turn left onto Aylesbury Street, go first right into St James's Walk and follow the road as it bears left into Sans Walk. On the right, you will find an unmarked pedestrian passageway, beneath which lie the remains of the House of Dentention.

The House of Detention

There has been a prison on this site since 1616, although the series of tunnels and passageways below ground level date from its last rebuilding in 1844. By the mid-19th century, the House of Detention, as it became known, was used as a holding prison for those awaiting trial, and an estimated 10,000 people a year passed through its gates. The prison was demolished in 1890, but an entire underground section survived and lay undisturbed until the bombs of the Blitz saw it reopened as an air-raid shelter. After World War II it was again largely forgotten until, in 1993, it became a museum. Sadly, the prison closed its doors to the public in the summer of 2000.

Many visitors to the prison used to pause here upon the threshold and find it an ordeal to step into the underground labyrinth. Even today, this nondescript little alleyway has a perpetual chill about it, and the tales of the many ghosts that lurk deep beneath your feet are sufficient to send many a shiver down the spine. Many visitors to the prison remarked on catching fleeting glimpses of a shadowy figure moving swiftly through the darkness ahead of them. Others would return from its dismal depths wondering who the old lady was who seemed to be desperately searching for something, but who would never respond to their offers of assistance. Several managers had been questioned by concerned visitors wanting to know about the little girl whose heart-rending sobs reverberated from the inner depths of

CLERKENWELL

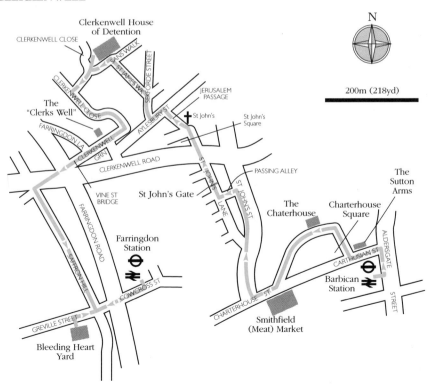

the jail. 'They genuinely believe that a lost child is wandering the dank maze of corridors and passageways', commented one member of staff before adding by way of explanation: 'Children were imprisoned here and the anguish they suffered must have been terrible. Perhaps this little girl's grief has somehow impregnated the stone and some people are just sensitive to that sort of thing.'

Well Court and Fagin's Lair

Leave the prison, go left into Clerkenwell Close, then turn right to follow the road as it takes you left and left again, pass the Church of St James Clerkenwell and go on to Clerkenwell Green. Turn right at the Crown Tavern and continue to Farringdon Lane where, beneath the office block, Well Court can be viewed. This is the remains of the clerk's well and an exhibition now details its history.

Go over Farringdon Lane into Vine Street Bridge and cross Farringdon Road at the traffic lights. Go left, then right over Clerkenwell Road and turn left into Saffron Hill. This was once a notorious London 'rookery', where criminals lived in vast sprawling tenements that overlooked the reeking waters of the various tributaries of the River Fleet. Dickens knew the area well and placed Fagin's lair here in *Oliver Twist*. Today the long road still has an eerie feel to it, dwarfed by massive office blocks and industrial units. Keep along it until you arrive at the junction with Greville Street, turn right and go first left into the aptly named Bleeding Heart Yard.

Bleeding Heart Yard

This stands on land occupied by the gardens of the Bishop of Ely's Palace, until Elizabeth I gave it all to her 'dancing chancellor' Sir Christopher Hatton.

Sir Christopher may well have danced many a May dance with his Virgin Queen, but his wife, Lady Hatton, chose to dance with the Devil and sold that worthy her soul. One night, as a great ball was in progress at Hatton House, the Devil came to collect. Robed in black, his head covered, he walked amongst the revellers until he found Lady Hatton, whom he led from the room. Suddenly the skies opened, there was a crash of thunder and a flash of bright lightning, and guests heard an ear-piercing scream from outside. Rushing to investigate, there was no sign of the mistress of the house except for:

> ... out in the courtyard – and just in that part
> where the pump stands – lay a bleeding Large Human Heart.

Go right along Greville Street, cross over Farringdon Road at the crossing and go straight ahead into Cowcross Street, to arrive at the end of the walk at Farringdon Underground Station. In 1758 thirteen-year-old Anne Naylor was murdered by the mother and daughter who ran a milliner's on the site now occupied by the station. Ever since, her terrified screams have been frequently heard echoing through the station, and are so loud that staff have dubbed her 'The Screaming Spectre'.

Lincoln's Inn Fields to Bloomsbury

Start	Holborn Underground Station (Central and Piccadilly lines)
Finish	Tottenham Court Road Underground Station (Central and Northern lines)
Distance	2¾ miles (4.4 kilometres)
Duration	2 hours
Best Time	The walk is best done on a weekday between 10am and 5pm.
Refreshments	The Ship Tavern and Dolphin Tavern, and numerous sandwich bars and cafés in Red Lion Street and Museum Street.

The walk proper begins at Lincoln's Inn Fields, where several monarchs exacted spiteful revenge on hapless subjects. It includes a visit to the Inns of Court, with a journey across the threshold of Lincoln's Inn, where barristers work and train. The walk crosses Red Lion Square, which is haunted by Oliver Cromwell. We step into the awesome interior of the British Museum to hear a chilling tale of a mummy's curse before finishing our ramble in the company of the 'most wicked man in the world'.

When passing through Lincoln's Inn Fields don't miss the opportunity to visit the fascinating Sir John Soane Museum, which is clearly signposted en route.

The Happy Ghost of the Ship Tavern

Leave Holborn Station and go left onto Kingsway, taking the left into Gate Street, at the end of which is located the Tavern.

During the despotic reign of Henry VIII, Catholics would sneak to this cosy, tucked-away hostelry and attend masses that were celebrated at the bar by outlawed priests. Look-outs would be posted around the neighbourhood, and a prearranged signal would warn the congregation when the king's zealous officials hove into view. The warning would give the priest sufficient time to escape into one of the pub's several 'hidey-holes', and the congregation time to take up their tankards and become just another group of pub regulars.

Listening as the king's officers searched for them, knowing that discovery would mean imprisonment, torture and certain death, those brave priests must have been shaking with fear. Crouched in the cramped confines of the hide, their hearts beating fast, their breath coming in short, sharp pants, they would have prayed hard for God to protect them; and an immense feeling of relief must have swept over those who, having evaded discovery, crept out of hiding and back among their flock. It is this aura of relief that pervades the atmosphere of the pub, and staff are extremely

LINCOLN'S INN FIELDS TO BLOOMSBURY

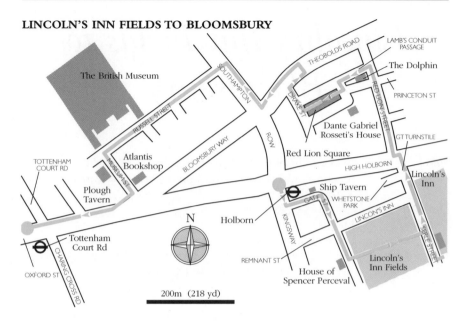

fond of their happy ghost. He never shows himself, but makes his presence known by mischievous pranks such as hiding cooking utensils for a few days or moving the cellar keys to other parts of the pub.

A Dream of Spencer Perceval

Follow Gate Street as it bears right and keep ahead over Remnant Street into Lincoln's Inn Fields. A little way along on the right you arrive at a salmon-coloured building where a dark plaque on the wall commemorates Spencer Perceval (1762–1812). The only English Prime Minister to have been assassinated, Perceval was gunned down in the lobby of the House of Commons by Liverpool greengrocer John Bellingham, who blamed him for the failure of his business. The story is remarkable for a well documented and authenticated dream that apparently foresaw the murder. On 3 May, 1812, John Williams, of Redruth in Cornwall, dreamt he was standing in the House of Commons when he saw a man in a brown coat draw a pistol and shoot a small man who was wearing a blue coat. He watched as a group of men overpowered the assassin and, when he was asked who had been shot, was told it was the chancellor. The same vivid dream was repeated three times and Williams wanted to leave immediately for London to warn Perceval. His family and friends, however, dissuaded him. On 12 May, news reached Cornwall that the Prime Minister had been assassinated the previous evening in the exact circumstances depicted by the dream. John Williams regretted to his dying day that he had not acted on the prophecy.

Gory Deaths in Lincoln's Inn Fields

Opposite the building, go through the gates and along the path that passes through the centre of Lincoln's Inn Fields. The massive trees that tower above you put

38

London's largest square in shimmering shadow. There is, however, nothing to commemorate the fact that, long ago, gruesome executions took place here. Sir Antony Babington and his Catholic followers had sworn to depose Elizabeth I and replace her on the throne of England with Mary Queen of Scots. When the plot was discovered in 1586, the fourteen conspirators were sentenced to be hanged, drawn and quartered over a period of two days, seven on one day and the remainder the next. Babington was still conscious when eviscerated, and endured untold agonies as his comrades looked on, knowing that they would soon face the same horrible fate. However, when Elizabeth heard of Babington's suffering, she decided on leniency and ordered that the remaining conspirators were to be hanged until dead before the disembowelling began. In 1683 William, Lord Russell was another to be executed here, for plotting against the life of Charles II. His wife, Lady Rachel Russell, pleaded with the king to reprieve her husband and spare his life. But Charles would not be moved. 'If I do not kill him, he will soon kill me,' he observed wryly. And so Russell came to his death in Lincoln's Inn Fields, observing philosophically that the pain of the axe would last for but a moment and cause him 'less pain than the drawing of a tooth'. Unfortunately the axe was wielded by the infamous and bungling Jack Ketch who, according to the diarist John Evelyn, 'took three butcherly strokes' to remove 'the patriot's' head, defending his crass ineptitude with the claim, "his Lordship moved".' Late at night, when the Fields are silent and empty, a shadowy dark figure is said to float about the shelter at the centre of the square and pain-racked screams are carried on the night breezes.

Lincoln's Inn and a Doppelgänger Tale

Continue ahead, turning right out of the garden where, on the left side, is the main entrance to Lincoln's Inn. Robert Perceval, cousin of Prime Minister Spencer, was a student at one of the prettiest of the four Inns of Court. However, unlike his illustrious and ill-fated relative, he fell into a dissolute lifestyle – of gambling, whoring and other vices – much to the detriment of his legal studies. Unusually, one night he was studying late in his chambers. He became strangely uneasy as the clock struck midnight. A cold shiver ran down his spine and, turning, he saw a shrouded figure that had somehow entered his locked room. He demanded to know its identity and purpose, but the figure made no reply and so Perceval picked up his sword and lurched at the mysterious spectre, only to see the blade pass straight through it. Terrified, he leapt at the figure and managed to uncover its face. He found himself looking at his own image, but with terrible gaping wounds about the face and chest. Seeing this as a warning that he must mend his wicked ways, he became a reformed character and for a while applied himself vigorously to his studies. But he soon tired of this and slipped back into his old ways, running up huge unsettled gambling debts. One morning his corpse was found sprawled in a gutter on the Strand. He had been run through with his own sword, his wounds being identical to those he had seen on the apparition.

Visit Lincoln's Inn on weekdays when its majestic courtyards and luxuriant gardens make a welcome and tranquil respite from the rush of modern London.

The Old Clock in the Dolphin

Leave the main gate and go right along Lincoln's Inn Fields to pass through Little Turnstile. Cross High Holborn at the pedestrian crossing. Turn left and then first right into Red Lion Street. Walk along the left pavement until, having crossed Princeton Street, you arrive on the left at the Dolphin. On 9 September, 1915, a Zeppelin bomb crashed onto the pub and reduced the building to a heap of smouldering rubble. Three customers were killed and several seriously injured in the tragedy. The clock was dragged from the rubble and now hangs, battered and scarred, to the left of the bar, its hands eerily frozen at 10.40pm, the exact moment when, on that night, death and destruction rained down from the heavens.

The pub today has a villagey feel to it, and is very much a 'local' in an area that has largely dedicated itself to catering for the needs of weekday office staff. But, when the last customer has gone home and the staff are busily tidying away the debris of another day, they occasionally feel their attention drawn inexplicably to the old clock and hear a soft mournful whistling that gets lower and lower until once more all is quiet.

The Posthumous Regicides of Red Lion Square

Immediately after visiting the Dolphin, go left along Lambs Conduit Passage, which opens onto Red Lion Square.

In 1660, Charles II returned from exile and the Restoration of the Monarchy was underway. Those loyal to the Royalist cause could look forward to rewards, while those who had supported the Parliamentarian campaign and allowed the beheading of Charles I could expect retribution now that a Stuart was again on the throne of England. But the three leading parliamentarians Oliver Cromwell, John Bradshaw and Henry Ireton were beyond the new king's reach. They lay buried in the hallowed earth of Westminster Abbey. Revenge was demanded and, on 29 January, 1661, the three were exhumed and tried for regicide. Though they had cheated the executioner in life, they would not do so in death. Found guilty, the bodies of Cromwell and Ireton rested overnight at the Red Lion Inn, which stood where the square is today, and at dawn the next day they were drawn on a hurdle to Tyburn, where they were joined by Bradshaw's putrefied corpse, and hanged by their necks until late afternoon. Cut down, the corpses had their heads hacked off and placed on spikes above Westminster Hall, while the bodies were flung into a deep pit and buried beneath the gallows.

Quite why their ghosts should haunt Red Lion Square is not certain, but haunt it they do. Deep in animated conversation, the three stroll purposefully and diagonally across the square where, once past the centre, they melt away little by little. Apart from ghostly regicides, the square has been home to other notable living residents. Jonas Hanway, who lived here, was a fearless trendsetter who ignored the jeers of his fellow citizens to become the first man to walk around the streets of London holding an umbrella. The Artist Dante Gabrielle Rossetti (1828–1882) is still commemorated by a plaque that adorns the wall of number 17. His landlord stipulated that 'the models are kept under some gentlemanly restraint as some artists sacrifice the dignity of art to the baseness of passion.'

Plate 1: The forbidding White Tower at the Tower of London. The many ghostly presences here include a 'White Lady' who drifts through the tower's rooms at night, her arrival signalled by her pungent perfume (see page 13).

Plate 2: Traitor's Gate at the edge of the Thames, through which passed many famous figures of history on their way to imprisonment and often execution in the Tower of London (see page 10).

Plate 3: *The infamous 'Beast of Whitechapel', otherwise known as Jack the Ripper, claims another victim in this contemporary print (see page 15).*

Plate 4: *No one apart from his wife was in St Botolph's Without Bishopsgate when Chris Brackley took this photograph. Yet a mysterious figure stands on the right-hand balcony (see page 22).*

Plate 5: *The Bank of England where the ghostly 'Old Lady in Black' still enquires after her executed brother (see page 24).*

Plate 6: *St Bartholomew the Great's old gatehouse (1595) around which agonised screams are said to rend the night air (see pages 30–31).*

Plate 7: 'Justice' atop the Old Bailey, built on the site of Newgate Prison (see page 28).

Plate 8: The house in Cock Lane, site of the 18th-century haunting by 'Scratching Fanny' (see page 34).

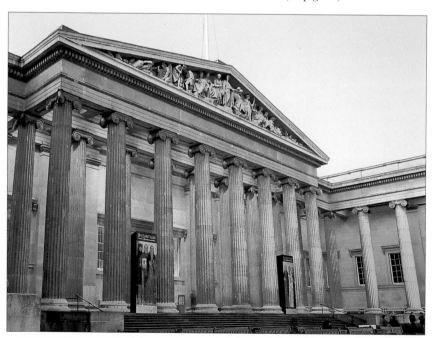

Plate 9: The British Museum, final resting-place of an Egyptian mummy which cursed all its previous owners (see page 41).

The British Museum and a Mummy's Curse

Go through the square and turn right onto Drake Street, then right onto Theobald's Road. Cross over the pedestrian crossing and bear left. At the end of Theobald's Road, turn right along Southampton Row, go over the crossing and into Bloomsbury Place. Follow this into Great Russell Street, where on the right is the museum.

The British Museum's most sinister and haunted section is to be found on the first floor, among the colourful sarcophagi and bandaged remains of the mummies in the Egyptian Rooms. In the second glass case to the right as you enter the first gallery are the grimacing remnants of Katebit, a priestess at the college of Amen Ra. It is said that those who look long and hard enough at the prostrate figure will occasionally see the head move from side to side.

But the exhibit with the most sinister history is the case captioned 'an unnamed singer of Amen-Re'. Richly decorated in colourful hieroglyphics, this mummy was originally purchased by three visitors to Thebes in the 1880s. Within a short time of its acquisition, one purchaser had been seriously injured in a shooting accident, another had mysteriously disappeared, and the third, fearing the curse, sold it to a dealer in antiquities. Three subsequent owners are said to have died in mysterious circumstances. It arrived in London in 1888, and was bought by a collector in Streatham. A medium advised him, 'Get rid of it or it will kill you.' Heeding the warning, he sold it to another antiquarian, whose attempts to have it photographed resulted in tragedy when his photographer died suddenly the next day. It was then sold to a lady collector, whose pets all died within two days of its purchase and so it was finally given to the British Museum. As it was being carried into the building by two porters, the curse struck again. One of the men tripped and broke his arm, and the other died a few days later. In 1921, two psychics performed an exorcism, releasing the casket's guardian spirit from its earthbound duties. Visitors can now safely enjoy its exquisite design without any danger of supernatural reprisals.

The Atlantis Bookshop

Leave the British Museum at Great Russell Street, cross over the pedestrian crossing, turn right, then left onto Museum Street. On the right is the Plough Tavern, once a favoured drinking haunt of Aleister Crowley (1875–1947), the self-proclaimed 'Great Beast', a man who delighted in making exaggerated claims involving the blood of virgins and Devil worship, and in the infamy that followed. At the end of the street on the left is the Atlantis Bookshop, founded in 1922 by Michael Houghton, and the oldest occult bookshop in London. Caroline Wise, the shop's enigmatic manageress, has experienced a few odd happenings since taking over in 1989. On more than one occasion she has caught a glimpse of a tall man in old-fashioned grey clothing rattling the rear door of the building, although he has never materialised in the shop. Her theory is that he is a previous owner of the building, returning to find the cause of the disturbance that the change of occupation has brought about. The shop stocks all manner of books covering a wide spectrum of esoteric, paranormal and occult subjects.

At the end of Museum Street go right and continue until you reach Tottenham Court Road Underground Station, where the walk ends.

Highgate

Start	Highgate Underground Station (Northern Line)
Finish	Archway Underground Station (Northern Line)
Distance	2½ miles (4 kilometres)
Duration	2 hours
Best Time	Any time, providing you can also take the scheduled tour of Highgate Cemetery.
Refreshments	The Gatehouse and The Flask Tavern both included on the walk.

This walk skirts the pleasing and atmospheric village of Highgate. Its hillside location affords spectacular views across the City of London. The first section of the walk is uneventful as far as ghosts are concerned, but its progress takes in picturesque and historic buildings. The section that descends the narrow, twisting Swain's Lane, lined by dark imposing walls and watched over by tall and sinister elm trees, is as spooky and sinister as you can get. The opportunity to join a scheduled guided tour through the overgrown pathways of Highgate Cemetery should not be missed.

Highgate High Level Station

Leave Highgate Underground Station from the Priory Gardens exit and go left to ascend the clearly defined, very steep path. Stop at the green barrier and look left into the cutting, where the remains of Highgate High Level Station can be seen hidden beneath some trees. Planned during World War II as an extension of the Northern Line, the station was left to the advance of creeping vegetation when the project was abandoned. It now nestles eerily in this deep cutting, from where the sounds of a ghost train, rumbling along non-existent tracks, are sometimes heard in the early hours of the morning.

Continue up the path and cross Wood Lane to turn right along Muswell Hill Road and arrive at No 10 Muswell Hill Road. In the late 1930s the actor Peter Sellers (1925–1980) lived here with his devoted and doting mother, Peg. Later in his life, after Peg had died, Sellers continued to be guided by her spirit, whose interference could prove costly to directors. Sellers insisted on expensive changes of location or seemingly needless delays to filming because of her ghostly advice.

The Gatehouse

Backtrack along the opposite side of Muswell Hill Road, cross over Archway and go along the left pavement of Southwood Lane. There follows a long walk which crosses Jackson's Lane and continues past Kingsley Place. From the corner there is a breathtaking view over the City of London. Pass the 1777 almshouses on the right until you come eventually to Highgate High Street. Cross over the pedestrian crossing and turn right. On the opposite side of the street the chapel of Highgate School rises majestically over a somewhat cluttered disused graveyard. Ahead of you stands the black and white timbered frontage of The Gatehouse. This rambling pub, rebuilt in 1905, is named for the gateway where travellers once paid tolls to cross land owned by the Bishop of London. It was this 'high gate' that gave its name to the village.

The pub is haunted by the 'ghost of Mother Marnes, an old lady murdered for her money inside the original gatehouse and whose appearances and ghostly activities can be terrifying. She only appears when there are no children or animals at the pub. One childless landlord was taken to hospital suffering from severe fright when she emerged from the shadows of the minstrel's gallery, now a theatre. 'I had gone up to switch off the gallery lights,' he recalled, 'when all of a sudden this thing appeared from nowhere. I can remember nothing else until waking up in hospital.' The walls are covered with pages of Highgate's history and interesting snippets about the pub itself. You can learn that Charles Dickens used to drink here and that the first cartoon to appear in *Punch* magazine was sketched at The Gatehouse.

The Ghost in the Flask
Leave the pub and go over the pedestrian crossing. Turn right along Highgate West Hill. The structure to your right is the reservoir that brought the first piped water to Highgate in 1854. At the end of the road, on the left, is the Flask, one of the area's most pleasing pubs. Dating from the early 18th century, this atmospheric old hostelry is a tranquil and timeless oasis that can number highwayman Dick Turpin and satirical artist William Hogarth among past customers. The pub adheres to many old customs such as The Swearing on the Horns. Participants in this ancient and venerated custom must kiss a pair of stag's antlers that dangle from a pole held before them and swear to drink only strong ale. The prize for the successful initiate is the freedom of Highgate, coupled with the right to kiss the most beautiful girl in the room.

That the Flask is haunted by a female entity is not disputed, although her identity is uncertain. Some say she is the lady whose sultry likeness hangs on the back wall of the main bar. Others claim she is the ghost of a former maidservant who killed herself following a failed love affair. Still others wonder if her demise and subsequent ghostly wanderings might be connected with the bullet that can still be seen embedded in the snug bar wall to the right of the entrance. When it was fired, at whom and by whom are questions that nobody can answer, and any connection with the haunting is convenient speculation.

Whoever she is, the staff always know when she is around because the temperature, even on a hot summer's day, begins to drop dramatically. Strange things happen. Lights swing back and forth, glasses move across tables in front of astonished customers, and some feel an unseen presence blowing onto the back of their necks. A clairvoyant who was once lunching at the pub with three friends suddenly told the manager they were leaving. She explained that, while the aura of the ghost was friendly, its presence was overwhelming and she found it quite disturbing. 'That ghost cost me four lunches,' lamented Andy, the manager.

Old Hall

Leave the Flask and turn left onto South Grove, passing the Old Hall on the right. This sturdy old mansion was built in 1691 on the site of Arundel House, where Sir Francis Bacon died. Statesman, philosopher, possible writer of the plays ascribed to Shakespeare – Bacon's talents and achievements were manifold. He was also a dabbler in scientific experiments, and had come to the conclusion that refrigeration might be a good way to preserve meat. On a bitterly cold morning in January 1626, in the company of his friend Doctor Winterborne, Bacon put his theory to the test. Purchasing a chicken from an old woman on Highgate Hill, he had it slaughtered and plucked, then stuffed the carcass with snow. By one of those ironic twists of justice with which the pages of history are littered, Bacon caught a severe chill as a result of the experiment, was rushed to Arundel House, placed in a damp bed and, within a short while, was dead.

The Phantom Chicken of Pond Square

Continue into South Grove and follow it into Pond Square, where the saga continues. The pond for which the square is named was filled in in 1864, and now there is a mass of unsightly asphalt surrounded by some delightful old buildings. Massive plane trees loom over the square and lend it an eerie, shadowy air. Late one night in 1943, one Terence Long was crossing the deserted square when he heard the sound of horses' hooves and the low rumble of carriage wheels. The next moment a loud raucous shriek split the silence and a huge white bird, like a plucked chicken, appeared from nowhere and began racing around in frenzied circles, flapping its wings. Long looked about him to see where it might have come from, and when he turned back the bird had vanished.

The phantom chicken has since paid several visits to Pond Square. It was seen in the 1960s by a motorist whose car had broken down and again in the 1970s by a courting couple saying their fond goodnights. On each occasion it dropped suddenly from above and gave a loud and distressed squeal, and strutted frantically round in a frenzied circle then disappeared.

The Restless Spirits of Highgate Cemetery

Just after the United Reformed Church, go right along Swain's Lane, which drops steeply between buildings of varying age. At the 'No Entry' sign, look through the rusting north gate of the cemetery. The mood has now changed considerably, with the high walls lending a peculiar claustrophobic atmosphere to the surroundings. Through the gate, narrow melancholy paths meander their way past sunken tombs that lean at weird angles, while angelic figures struggle to free themselves from an abundance of creeping vegetation and undergrowth. A dark figure is often seen moving swiftly among these graves, while a hideous grey face scowling from the other side of the gates has distressed many who walk this way in the fading light of early evening. Its gnarled fingers grip the rusting ironwork and its hollow sunken eyes are fixed in a grimacing stare as it watches and waits for its victims to turn on their heels and race to the safety of the village.

Continue along Swain's Lane, which twists and turns between dark walls, the

HIGHGATE

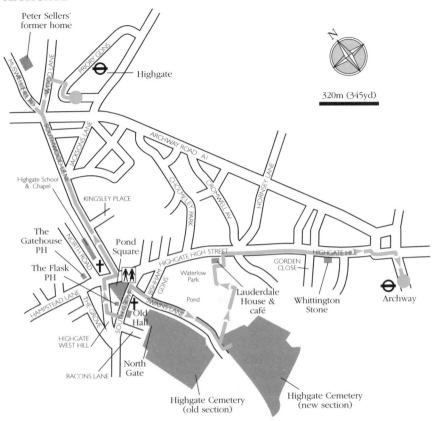

gradient becoming steeper with each step you take. When the road widens you find yourself standing between the two sections of Highgate Cemetery. The older section on the right can be visited only on guided tours conducted by the enthusiastic Friends of Highgate Cemetery, whose response to questions about ghosts and the supernatural is decidedly unfriendly.

Sprawled across seventeen grassy, hillside acres, and opened in 1839, this became the most sought-after burial spot in London, and fashion-conscious Victorians wouldn't be seen dead in any other necropolis. By the dawn of the 20th century, nearly 100,000 people, many of them famous and illustrious, had been laid to rest here. Ambitious tombs were built as families struggled to outdo each other with more and more ostentatious resting places for their loved ones. But then came World War II and a severe downturn in the cemetery's fortunes. The once-proud tombs fell into disrepair. Decay and neglect crept unchecked, as the roots of tangled shrubbery split apart once-magnificent graves and left their masonry sprawled and contorted across toppled columns, while decaying fragments of broken urns spewed across the twisting pathways.

Rumours began to circulate that strange ceremonies were being held after dark in the abandoned ruins. The local newspaper, the *Hampstead and Highgate Express,* began to receive letters from readers telling of ghostly activity around the gates of the cemetery. One unfortunate man, whose car broke down in Swain's Lane, suddenly noticed a terrible and frightful apparition glaring at him through the bars of the gate. Another man found himself knocked to the ground by something that 'seemed to glide' from the cemetery. He was saved when the headlights of an approaching car caused the spectre to 'dissolve into the cemetery wall'. On Friday 27 February, 1970, the front-page headline of the *Hampstead and Highgate Express* posed the question: 'DOES A VAMPIRE WALK IN HIGHGATE?' It was followed a week later with: 'WHY DO THE FOXES DIE? The mysterious death of foxes in Highgate Cemetery was this week linked with the theory that a ghost seen in the area might be a vampire.'

Thus began a period of intense media interest, with camera crews flocking to the cemetery hoping to catch the vampire on film. Vampire hunters, occultists and the curious swarmed around the grim mausoleums, garlic and crucifixes poised to ward off the evil. More and more letters telling of frightening meetings with ethereal forms in the vicinity of Swain's Lane graced the pages of the local newspaper. A ghostly cyclist panting and puffing his way up the steep incline had terrified a young mother, and tales were told of a tall man in a hat who would walk across Swain's Lane and disappear through the wall into the cemetery. Local superstition maintained that the bells in the old disused chapel would toll whenever he walked.

Cross Swain's Lane and pay an admission charge so that you can wander freely through the newer east cemetery. Although not as creepy as its western counterpart, it is nonetheless atmospheric. A small booklet giving directions to the last resting place of many famous names, including the novelist George Eliot and the philosopher Karl Marx, can be purchased at the gate.

The ghost of a mad old woman, her long grey hair streaming behind her, is said to move at great speed among the graves here. She is supposedly looking for the resting place of her children, whom she murdered in a fit of insane rage. She shares her ghostly domain with a shrouded figure that gazes pensively into space, apparently oblivious to those who see it unless they get too close, whereupon it vanishes, only to reappear a little further away, still adopting the same listless, meditative pose.

Lauderdale House

Backtrack along Swain's Lane a little way and then go right through the gates of Waterlow Park. Follow the path as it sweeps left, then take the right fork and go over the bridge. Follow the path that ascends to the left, take the left fork, go up the hill and turn left along the pathway and go up the steps on the right, which are surmounted on either side by two headless eagles.

At the central circle, cross left to the steps up to the house, which was built in 1580 and in the 17th century modernised by the Earl of Lauderdale. He lent it to Charles II as a hideaway for his mistress, Nell Gwyn. Anxious for their baby son to be granted a title, Nell is said to have dangled the boy by his legs from an upstairs window and threatened to drop the child unless the king did something for him. 'So be it,' sighed Charles. 'Save the Earl of Burford.'

Leave Lauderdale House by the Highgate Hill exit (you may like to turn left and walk into Highgate Village High Street), turn right and descend this unattractive thoroughfare (which does, however, offer a superb view across London). Some way down you pass the Whittington Stone, marking the site where Dick Whittington is said to have heard the bells of Bow Church urging him to turn again. Atop the stone sits a sleepy-looking stone cat casting a wary backward glance at the city below. Continue your descent of the hill to arrive at Archway Station, where the walk ends.

Hampstead

Start/Finish	Hampstead Underground Station (Northern Line)
Distance	3.5 miles (5.6 kilometres)
Duration	2½ hours
Best Time	Any time, although St John's Church is closed after dark, a time when I wouldn't recommend venturing onto the Heath anyway.
Refreshments	The Holly Bush Hotel, Spaniards Inn and the Flask Tavern. Hampstead High Street offers many pleasing restaurants and cafeterias.

Hampstead is a delightful village perched on a hill 440 feet (135 metres) above sea level. There has been a settlement here for over a thousand years and from the Middle Ages ônwards Londoners journeyed here to take the air, enjoy the fresh water or escape the plague raging in the city below. It was the arrival of poets such as Keats and Shelley and the artists Constable and Romney that helped establish Hampstead as a Bohemian village. Today it is still home to actors, film stars and writers. This walk is a relatively long one that begins with a stroll through the bustling village centre before striking off into the back streets in search of vampires and ghosts.

Much of the walk is spent crossing Hampstead Heath, which even today can be lonely, desolate and, if the conditions are right, quite frightening. Highlights include the eerie overgrown pathways of St John's Church and a chance to unwind and seek out the ghosts at the splendid Spaniards Inn, once a haunt of highwayman Dick Turpin.

A Haunted Pub

Leave Hampstead Underground Station, go left along Hampstead High Street, use the pedestrian crossing and continue left to the William IV.

This quintessential Hampstead pub is cosy, snug and haunted. Local tradition maintains that a long time ago a doctor's wife, for reasons long since forgotten, was murdered by her husband and bricked up in the lower depths of the house, now the pub's cellar. Ever since, her ghost has rattled windows and slammed doors in the middle of the night, and generally disturbed the pub.

This section of the High Street is haunted by the ghost of a young girl who stands on the pavement looking sadly in at the windows of the pub. She wears a white shroud and her long plaited hair hangs untidily across her shoulders. She is said to be the phantom of a patient at a dental practice that once stood opposite.

Following a particularly traumatic bout of oral treatment, the poor girl killed herself rather than keep her next appointment.

Church Row and Dracula's Victim

Go right along Perrin's Lane, where the quaint brick cottages lining the right side contrast sharply with the modern buildings on the left. Go right onto Heath Street and cross via the pedestrian crossing, keeping ahead into Church Row. The graceful approach to the parish church was built in the 18th century and is considered the most attractive street in Hampstead. The writer William Makepeace Thackeray's daughter Anne described it as 'an avenue of Dutch, red-faced houses, leading demurely to the old church tower that stands, guarding its graves in the flowery churchyard'.

One of the houses near the church is reputed to have been the scene of the gruesome murder of a small child in the latter half of the 19th century. The murderer, a red-haired maidservant, dismembered the body and smuggled the remains out of the house in a carpet bag. People walking along Church Row as the first rays of daylight appear have heard stealthy footsteps shuffling behind them and a red-haired woman has been seen moving quickly toward the church, her head turning from side to side as she glances furtively around her.

Follow her ghostly route: go through the gates of the Parish Church of St John, and turn immediately left to descend the earth path that snakes its way past crumbling, weatherworn tombs. As it twists violently right and the ground beneath your feet changes to asphalt, you pass the tomb of the artist John Constable (1776–1837). Walk to the end of that path, go right and take the right uphill fork, passing beneath gigantic trees that give a shadowy stillness as you walk among the graves.

It has been suggested that this was the churchyard in which Bram Stoker (1847–1912) placed the vault that housed the undead Lucy Westenra in *Dracula*. The location is certainly eerie and sinister, and it is easy to imagine Van Helsing and Dr Seward standing by the tomb which 'in the daytime, and when wreathed with fresh flowers, had looked grim and gruesome enough; but now, some days afterwards, when the flowers hung lank and dead, their whites turning to rust and their greens to browns; when the spider and the beetle had resumed their accustomed dominance... was more miserable and sordid than could have been imagined...' A few days later they return, accompanied by Arthur Holmwood, and it is he who dispatches the vampire in time-honoured fashion as he takes the wooden stake, places the point over the heart and strikes with all his energy. 'The thing in the coffin writhed; and a hideous blood-curdling screech came from the opened red lips. The body shook and quivered and twisted in wild contortions; the sharp white teeth champed together till the lips were cut and the mouth was smeared with a crimson foam. But Arthur never faltered... his untrembling arm rose and fell, driving deeper and deeper the mercy-bearing stake, whilst the blood from the pierced heart welled and spurted up around it... And then the writhing and quivering of the body became less. Finally it lay still. The Terrible task was over...'

Keep ahead along the path and, on arrival at the church (well worth a visit), go straight ahead and out of the side gate to cross the road into Holy Walk. Once past the extension of the overgrown churchyard that lines the right side, you pass pretty Blenheim Place. The trim cottages that line the route date from 1813. Further on is the Catholic Church of St Mary's, built in 1796 by and for refugees who fled their homeland during the French Revolution. Further on, a plaque on the wall at the junction with Holly Berry Lane commemorates the site of Hampstead's first Police Station.

Turn right into Mount Vernon where, at Number 7, Robert Louis Stevenson (1850–1894), author of *Dr Jekyll and Mr Hyde, Treasure Island* and many others, lodged on several occasions.

The Holly Bush Inn: Service from the Ghost with a Smile

At the end of Mount Vernon go immediately left along the narrow twisting pathway, cross over Holly Hill and keep ahead into Holly Mount, where on the left is the Holly Bush Inn.

This gaslit, atmospheric old inn was once frequented by Boswell and Doctor Johnson. It also has associations with the painter George Romney, whose house still stands nearby. It was the stables of the house that became the Holly Bush Inn. The pub once had a long musical tradition, with jazz being played there on Sunday nights for many, many years. About forty years ago it was customary for a certain band leader to reward the pianist at the end of a performance with an encouraging slap on the back, a tradition still carried on by an unseen hand that the current piano player has felt across his back on several occasions.

If you choose to eat at the pub, and a waitress wearing a crisp white linen apron and a long dark skirt takes your order, don't blame the staff if you have a long wait. 'We don't offer waitress service,' says landlord Peter Dures. 'People come up to the bar and order.' Yet on more than one occasion Peter and his wife, Hazel, have found themselves confronted by irate customers, demanding to know why their lunch is taking so long to arrive. It transpires that they have given their order to a phantom waitress who, although very polite and obliging, never delivers the orders to the kitchen!

Go right out of the pub and turn right onto Holly Bush Hill. Number 5 was the home and studio of George Romney (1734–1802). Keep ahead into Hampstead Grove and pass Fenton House, Hampstead's oldest mansion (*c.*1693) and now home to the Benton Fletcher collection of early keyboard instruments. Go left into Admiral's Walk, pass on the right the Admiral's House, notable for its roof, which resembles a ship's quarterdeck. It was adapted in 1791 by the then occupant, Lieutenant Fountain North, who used to fire a cannon from his roof to celebrate royal birthdays. Next door, at Grove Lodge, John Galsworthy (1867–1933), author of the *Forsyte Saga*, lived.

At the end of Admiral's Walk, go right onto Lower Terrace, over the grass triangle in the centre of the road, straight across into the unnamed walkway to the right of the line of pretty cottages (number 2 was the summer residence of John Constable and his family) and make your way to the open space that can be seen ahead. Go through the gap in the railings onto Judges' Walk, traditionally held to be the place where justices came to take the air after they had fled London during the Great Plague of 1665.

HAMPSTEAD

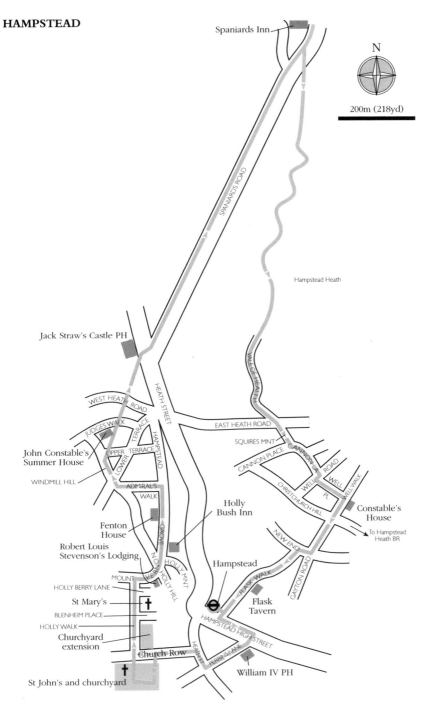

Spaniards Inn

N

200m (218yd)

Hampstead Heath

Jack Straw's Castle PH

WEST HEATH ROAD

HEATH STREET

JUDGES WALK

UPPER TERRACE

LOWER TERRACE

TERRACE

HAMPSTEAD

EAST HEATH ROAD

VALE OF HEALTH

SQUIRES MNT

CANNON PLACE

CANNON LA

ROAD

John Constable's Summer House

WINDMILL HILL

ADMIRAL'S WALK

CHRISTCHURCH HILL

WELL

PL

WELL WALK

Holly Bush Inn

Constable's House

To Hampstead Heath BR

Fenton House

GROVE

NEW END

Robert Louis Stevenson's Lodging

MOUNT

HOLLY HILL

HOLLY MNT

VERNON

Hampstead

GAYTON ROAD

FLASK WALK

HOLLY BERRY LANE

St Mary's

Flask Tavern

BLENHEIM PLACE

HOLLY WALK

HAMPSTEAD HIGH STREET

Churchyard extension

Church Row

HEATH ST

PERRINS LANE

William IV PH

St John's and churchyard

Jack Straw's Castle

Keep ahead along the rough pathway and bear right across the open Heath, then cross Lower Terrace and bear left to cross the busy main roads towards the large yellow, weatherboard building at the corner of North End Way. This was Jack Straw's Castle, a pub that was completely rebuilt following bomb damage in World War II. It was another favoured haunt of Charles Dickens, who spent many a happy hour at what he termed 'a good 'ouse' enjoying a 'red hot chop for dinner'. Van Helsing and Dr Seward dined here before their midnight vigil at Lucy's tomb. 'Jack Straw' was a generic name for farm labourers, and this was reputedly the rallying point for Hampstead labourers on their way to join Wat Tyler's peasant revolt in 1381.

Spaniards Inn

Cross the pedestrian crossing outside the pub, go past the war memorial and bear left into Spaniards Road. A long walk follows, the monotony of which is occasionally broken by stunning views to the right across Hampstead Heath and over London beneath. Eventually you arrive at Spaniards Inn. This 16th-century hostelry was named for two Spanish brothers, joint proprietors who argued over a woman and killed each other in a duel.

Following this inauspicious start, the pub later became a reputed haunt of highwayman Dick Turpin, who stabled his mount, Black Bess, here. Her ghostly hoof beats are still heard galloping across the car park in the dead of night. Turpin himself has been seen inside the pub – a shadowy, cloaked figure that strides purposefully across the bar then disappears into the wall. On the panelled first floor is Turpin's Bar, where, in winter months, a roaring log fire crackles in an ancient fireplace, and customers have often felt an unseen hand tugging gently at their sleeves. Leave the pub and backtrack along Spaniards Lane, but keep to the left side. On arrival at the wide drive, bear left along the earth pathway and follow it as it curves left and twists, then descends steeply through scrub. Keep ahead over the pathway, passing the communications mast, and go right on a tortuous route that runs through the gorse parallel to the main road then drops steeply left downhill, and becomes very lonely and desolate. Two hundred years ago, this journey would have been undertaken only by the brave or the foolhardy. Records show dozens of attacks on travellers, many ending with murder. Even today you get the uncanny feeling that someone is watching from the dense woodland and bushes, waiting to pounce upon you at any moment.

Worse still is the ghostly, dark figure on horseback that comes riding from the thickets towards walkers. He has been seen by many people, including a Mrs Helen Steipel, who was so convinced she was about to be trampled to death by the horse's hooves that she flung herself onto the muddy ground and waited for the impact. When nothing happened, she looked up to find both the rider and his mount had vanished. Only then did it dawn on her that, despite the apparent great speed at which they were travelling, there had been no sound from the horse's hooves.

At the gravel path, go left. Follow the path to the right and descend the asphalt path on the right. Keep ahead until you reach a barrier and there turn right into the Vale of Health. This sleepy Hampstead corner acquired its picturesque name in 1802, when a malodorous, malarial swamp was drained to make way for the construction of numerous fashionable dwellings.

Go left after Byron Villas and keep ahead to cross over East Heath Road. A grinning, toothless old man in a brown Norfolk jacket has been known to follow pedestrians along this stretch of road. So real does he appear that the first hint of his being anything more than living flesh and blood is his abrupt disappearance.

The Flask Tavern
Cross East Heath Road and go along Squire's Mount. At the junction with Cannon Place is Cannon Hall, childhood home of the writer Daphne du Maurier (1907–1989). Passing the old cannon that serve as street bollards, descend Cannon Lane. On the right, some way down, is the 18th-century lock-up, whose history is detailed on a wall plaque.

Cross Well Road, and take the small pathway directly opposite, turning right along Well Walk. Opposite is number 40, where John Constable lived from 1827 until his death ten years later. Cross Christchurch Hill, and keep ahead into Flask Walk, which ends at a paved passage, on the left of which is the tavern.

This cosy old pub takes its name from the flasks that in the 18th century were sold here, to those who came to take the waters at the nearby springs. It is haunted by a 19th-century landlord called Monty. A stickler for tradition, and totally opposed to change, he keeps a close eye on those who are now entrusted with the running of his pub. The 1997 redevelopment of the conservatory caused him considerable annoyance and he disrupted the work as often as he could. Upon its completion he made his disdain apparent by moving tables across the floor in front of astonished customers, and by switching off the lights.

At the end of the alley is Hampstead High Street where, to the right, is Hampstead Underground Station, which is where the walk ends.

Enfield

Location	11 miles (17.7 kilometres) north of Charing Cross
Transport	Enfield Chase can be reached from Cockfosters Underground Station (Piccadilly Line). However, do bear in mind that the sites are very spread out.
Refreshments	Various pubs are dotted around the outer perimeter of Enfield Chace.

The random and spread-out nature of the hauntings in Enfield makes it difficult to devise a satisfactory route, and the haunted sites are simply marked on the accompanying map to allow you to visit them at your leisure. The majority are centred around Enfield Chace, and a morning or afternoon spent walking its green expanse is a richly rewarding experience. Historically, Enfield Town is a fascinating and, in parts, picturesque place to explore, and I strongly recommend that you incorporate the Enfield Walk from Andrew Duncan's *Village London* (1997) into your exploration of the area's more sinister and ethereal aspects.

1. Bell Lane, Enfield

On a cold, crisp December evening in 1961 young Robert Bird was cycling along Bell Lane on his way to a Boy's Brigade meeting. In the distance he caught sight of two lights, about an arm's length apart, approaching from the opposite direction. As they got closer they suddenly veered to his side of the road and he realised that they were heading straight for him. Convinced he was about to be hit by an out-of-control vehicle, Robert tried to get out of its way but its approach was too fast, and as it thundered towards him, he tensed and prepared for the impact. As it got closer he saw to his surprise that it was a black coach, driven by two shadowy figures, pulled by four horses and travelling four or five feet above the ground. He was even more amazed when the apparition simply passed straight through him and, as he turned to look, vanished.

Robert Bird was the last in a long line of witnesses to the ghostly journey of the 'Phantom Coach of Enfield' that races along this stretch of road with its wheels above the ground, although their noise and that of the horses' hooves can be clearly heard. Local tradition dates the spectral sight to the 18th century, when this was a marshy, inhospitable area and the road was a good deal higher than it is today. It wasn't uncommon for drivers to lose control and for their coaches to career off the road, bringing at best inconvenience and at worst a watery, slow death to their passengers. Did Robert and other witnesses see the final journey of one such coach that for some reason is now reenacted?

2. Camlet Moat, Enfield Chace

This is a heavily wooded area, where muddy paths wind their way through skeleton-like trees and where, even on bright summer days, a strange coolness hangs in the air and the woodland is shadowy and eerie. In the distant past, this land was owned by the De Mandeville family, and legend tells how one member of the family found himself under suspicion of treason. Realising that his fortune would be forfeit should he be found guilty and executed, he packed his treasure into a strong chest and lowered it into a deep well. Today, it is covered by dense thickets. Once his treasure was hidden, he hid in the branches of a great oak that stood alongside the well and watched for the approach of his enemies. But one day he lost his balance, tumbled headlong from the tree and was killed. Since then many have tried to retrieve his vast fortune but none have succeeded. When the chest is hauled near to the brink, the chain holding it always snaps and sends it plummeting back into the darkness. Others have spoken of walking in the woods as evening falls and becoming aware of a tall figure, clad in shining armour, standing some distance away, watching them with intense suspicion. It is De Mandeville, still guarding the treasure for which he gave his life all those centuries ago.

3. Hadley Road, Enfield

The 17th century was a harsh and cruel time for those who lived around the desolate Enfield Chace. Plague was a frequent visitor to these isolated communities, and livestock would die suddenly. Seemingly robust children would perish under the sudden onslaught of mysterious illnesses. Crops would wither and rot, bringing untold financial hardship. Healthy men and women succumbed to the "wasting disease". No matter what the tragedy, the victims were always certain that the cause was witchcraft.

A witch who lived in an isolated hovel on this stretch of the chase was executed in 1622. But, when the moon is full and the mists swirl across the road, she returns as a stooped and gnarled old hag, dressed in black and hobbling along slowly and painfully.

4. Old House at the Top of Oak Avenue

On 5 April, 1873, Mr J.Weserfield, a local solicitor, came to dine with two spinster sisters who lived in an old house at the top of Oak Hill. They warmly welcomed him and showed him to a bedroom where he could change for dinner. No sooner had he taken off his jacket than he became aware of a strange noise, a peculiar, trembling sigh that sounded immediately beside him. Thinking it to be nothing more than the wind in the chimney, he continued dressing, only to hear the sound again, but this time it was louder. From then on he became aware of a presence that followed him wherever he went in the room and which emitted tormented sounds every few minutes. He finished dressing as quickly as he could and raced from the room to join the two sisters at the dinner table. But for the whole evening the presence stayed with him, and it wasn't until he had left the house that he felt free of its influence. When he next met the two sisters he told them of his experience. They simply laughed and told him that they and others who had

ENFIELD

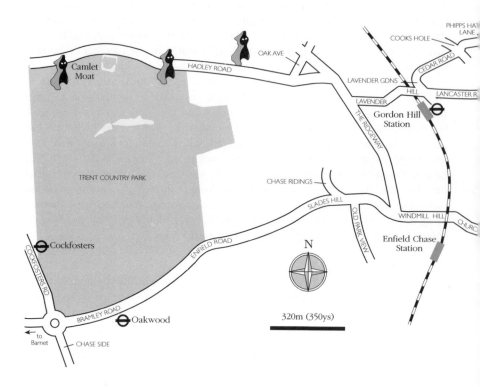

come to visit had often felt and heard the ghostly resident, though no one knew who or what it was or even why it should have chosen to take up its ghostly occupancy in that particular room.

5. The Rose and Crown, Clay Hill
The ghost of Dick Turpin must be one of the busiest in England! For that matter, with the number of pubs that claim his living self as a previous customer, it's a miracle he was able to stay upright in the saddle! The Rose and Crown on Clay Hill was kept by Turpin's grandfather 'Mr Mott' and local tradition maintains that the highwayman would hide at the pub to evade capture if the king's officers got close to him. His ghost is said to haunt not only the pub but also the road outside, where, astride a huge and fearsome phantom 'Black Bess', he gallops through the night, en route, perhaps, to one of the many other pubs he has to haunt.

6. The Enfield to Barnet Road
The sun had sunk beneath the horizon and the autumn night was closing in as Mr Ward and his uncle travelled home along the Enfield to Barnet Road. All was quiet and still, the only sound being the steady clatter of the horses' hooves and the

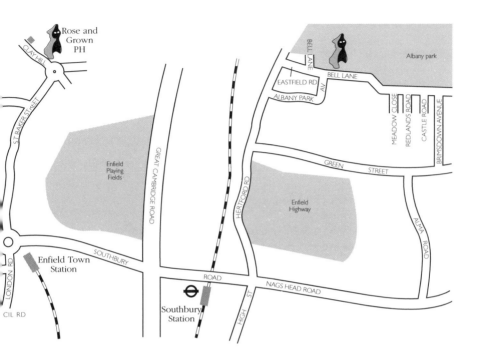

low rumbling of the carriage wheels. As the night shadows deepened and the trees became more shadowy with each passing moment, a feeling of sudden terror, followed by an intense melancholy, descended upon both men. Moments later the horses shied in alarm and, without any warning, bolted. The carriage was dragged at breakneck speed as Mr Ward struggled to control the terrified animals.

Then the moon suddenly burst from behind a bank of cloud and, as its silver light illuminated the scene, both men saw the cause of the horses' alarm. Walking on the grass verge alongside them, keeping up easily with the animals' speed, was a tall man with a deathly white face. A deep, gaping wound across one side of his throat glimmered eerily in the moonlight.

On they galloped until, as they rounded a bend, the hideous phantom fell behind and stopped by a certain gate. The horses became calmer, their speed slackened, and, when the two men looked back, they saw the figure standing by the gate staring after them. But as they watched, it began to fade and moments later vanished.

The next day Mr Ward was telling a friend of the experience and learnt that in 1832 a Mr Danby had been murdered by that gate. It was well known in the locality that his ghost still walked the lane where the crime had occurred.

Great Portland Street to Theatreland

Start	Great Portland Street Underground Station (Circle, Hammersmith & City and Metropolitan lines)
Finish	Piccadilly Circus Underground Station(Bakerloo and Piccadilly lines)
Distance	2 miles (3.2 kilometres)
Duration	1¼ hours
Best Time	Early on a Sunday morning, when the area is relatively uncrowded
Refreshments	The Argyle Arms in Argyle Street is highly recommended. The route is lined by numerous pubs and sandwich bars.

This varied walk starts with the graceful splendour of a crescent designed by the architect John Nash (1752–1835) and moves on to hauntings at the BBC. You will encounter the frenzied rush of Regent Street, then step back to a more graceful age, amid the Regency splendour of Burlington Arcade. Next are the Queen's grocer, a graceful Wren Church and an elegant square; then the route ends at one of London's most sumptuous theatre frontages. Highlights en route include the opportunity to visit the BBC and to undertake a tour of the London Palladium, a stroll along Carnaby Street and the chance to window-shop in London's most exclusive shopping arcade.

Leave Great Portland Street Station, turn left onto Marylebone Road, continue over the traffic lights and then turn left into Park Crescent. Follow the gracious curve of this elegant thoroughfare, designed originally by John Nash and completely rebuilt following the damage inflicted upon it during World War II. At the red pillar box go left into Portland Place (named for Hans Bentinck [1649–1709] a favourite of William III who was given the title Earl of Portland in 1689), the width of which was dictated by Lord Foley. He owned a house at the south end, and stipulated that he must have an uninterrupted northward view from his house in perpetuity. Nash complied by making Portland Place as wide as his lordship's house was long.

Encounters in the Langham Hotel

Continue the length of Portland Place until you arrive at the pedestrian crossing that goes over to the hotel that stands on the site of Lord Foley's mansion. The house was acquired by John Nash in settlement of a debt, and the land was sold to Sir James Langham for a new town house on condition that Nash could build it. Then in 1864 the Langham Hotel, forerunner of London's grand hotels, was built on the site. To its Victorian splendour came Toscanini, Mark Twain, Arnold Bennett, Napoleon III of France and Haile Selassie. The composer Dvořák was another guest, although he scandalised the management when, in an attempt to save money, he requested a double bedroom for himself and his grown-up daughter.

As grander hotels were built, the Langham's popularity declined, and by the 1950s it was being used as administrative offices by the BBC. Several rooms on the third floor were kept as accommodation for staff to stay overnight. In 1973, announcer James Alexander Gordon was sleeping over in Room 333. He awoke in the middle of the night to see a fluorescent ball floating on the opposite side of the room. As he watched, it began to take on the form of an Edwardian gentleman in full evening dress. Scared half out of his wits, Gordon summoned up the courage to ask, in a nervous voice, who it was and what it wanted. The question seemed to irritate the spectre, for it began to float toward him, arms outstretched, eyes gazing, fixed and unblinking. Alexander rushed from the room. Later, when he told his colleagues at Broadcasting House about the experience, others told of similar experiences in that same bedroom.

The Ghosts of Broadcasting House

Go back over the zebra crossing and pause outside Broadcasting House. Built to provide twenty-two soundproof studios for the BBC, it remains largely unaltered since being first occupied, on 2 May, 1932. The figures above the main doorway were sculpted by Eric Gill (1882–1940) and show Shakespeare's Ariel, as a symbol of broadcasting, being sent out into the world by Prospero.

In 1937 the figure of a man was seen limping about the fourth floor of the building. He wore old-fashioned clothes and sported fine, twirling whiskers. So real did he look that witnesses took him to be a senior member of management until, to their astonishment, he began to dissolve before their eyes. Other ghosts seen here have included a spectral waiter, who wanders the corridors, and a musician who appears to be lost. When people approach to offer help, he responds by shaking his head and vanishing.

Walk along Langham Street, turn right onto Great Portland Street and keep ahead until you arrive on the right at The Cock public house. Although he has never seen or experienced the ghost, the landlord, Campbell Scott Mackay, always knows when it is about because his dog begins to get nervous and refuses to go anywhere near the cellar of the pub.

The London Palladium Wraith

Continue along Great Portland Street, go over Oxford Street and then turn right off the pedestrian crossing to take the first left into Argyle Street. Go halfway along. Opened in 1910 and officially named The London Palladium in 1934, the theatre gave its first suggestion of being haunted in March 1973 when a doorkeeper revealed the existence of the ghost during a television interview.

Located at the rear of the Royal Circle is the old Crimson Staircase, said to be a leftover from the 18th-century Argyll House that formerly stood on the site. A spectral lady in a crinoline dress glides gracefully past those who are ascending the stairs. She has been seen by theatre hands, usherettes and even visiting artistes, although nobody can be sure who she was. A possible contender is Mrs Shireburn, mistress of the Duke of Argyll, who lived in the house 1750–62. Perhaps the sound of the orchestra, the rustling of the audience or the adrenaline-charged air of the stage during a performance is what attracts her.

Continue to the end of Argyle Street, go left into Great Marlborough Street, cross at the pedestrian crossing, and go left and then first right into Carnaby Street where, a little way along, you arrive at the Shakespeare's Head pub. A board on the wall gives a detailed history, and above that sits a rather hollow-eyed, dejected looking bard, no doubt bemoaning the loss of his writing hand, blown off by a bomb during the Blitz.

GREAT PORTLAND STREET
TO THEATRELAND

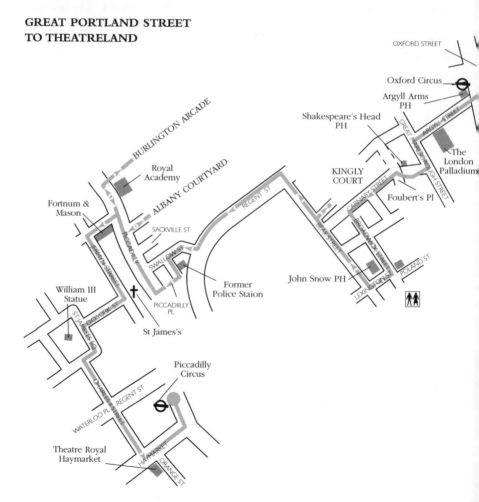

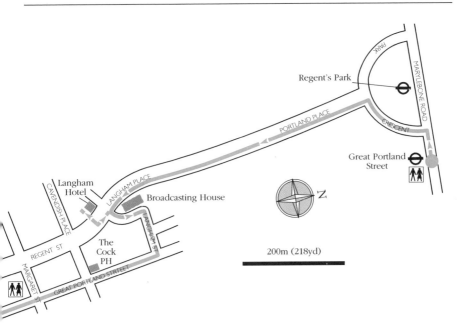

Regent's Park

Great Portland
Street

Langham
Hotel

Broadcasting House

The
Cock
PH

200m (218yd)

The John Snow Public House

Walk along Carnaby Street, the centre of 'swinging London' in the 1970s, and take the third turning on the left into Broadwick Street. Keep ahead, and on the right you will find the John Snow public house. Located on a busy Soho corner, this dark, tiny pub commemorates the man who proved that cholera is a waterborne disease. During the epidemic that swept London in 1854, Snow (1813–1858) plotted on a map the addresses of 500 people who had died that September. He noted that the Broad Street (as Broadwick Street was then called) pump was at the geographic centre of the epidemic. His theory, that polluted drinking water caused the disease, met with widespread disbelief. To prove his theory, Snow removed the handle of the pump, rendering it unusable, and the outbreak ended soon afterwards.

Across from the pub, at the junction with Poland Street, is a modern replica of the pump on which can be read an account of Snow's activities, while a large board on the pub's staircase goes into great detail about the good doctor himself.

Just who haunts the pub is not known. Some say that a shadowy figure sits in the far corner of the bar, its ghastly red eyes staring into space and a horrible pain-racked grimace contort its features. The manager, James Rookes, has often been sitting in his office counting the day's takings when he has felt somebody walk behind him, only to turn to find that he is alone.

Leave the pub and turn right into Lexington Street, a dark, narrow thoroughfare, then go right into Beak Street and walk to Kingly Court. This dismal, drab passageway is sometimes visited by a man in 18th-century dress who is seen strolling back and forth, stroking his chin meditatively, or on occasion whistling tunelessly to himself.

The Spectral Sergeant of Vine Street Police Station

Continue to the end of Beak Street, cross over the pedestrian crossing and go left along Regent Street. Walk to the stone arch that you can see on the right some way ahead, and go through it into Swallow Street. Go first left into Vine Street, and pause outside the second building on the left, which was the police station.

In the early years of the 20th century, a sergeant working one evening at the police station stepped into a cell, removed his belt and hanged himself from the back of the door. The reason for his suicide was never established, but reports that his ghostly form was haunting the building began to circulate during World War II, when the Aliens' Registration Office moved here. Staff would hear the distinctive sound of heavy boots clumping across the floors of the basement. One person even saw a figure in an old-fashioned police uniform looking into the cell in which the officer died.

When the building once more reverted to the Metropolitan Police, the ghost in blue became even more active. Several officers complained that their documents were being rearranged by an unseen hand. Others spoke of cell doors being mysteriously opened during the night.

The police have now moved and, at the time of writing, the building remains empty. But on occasion, standing in the creepily drab Vine Street as the shadows of night descend, you might just hear the sound of heavy boots striding briskly over cold stone as the ghostly sergeant pounds his spiritual beat.

Albany

Go through the barriers opposite, walk down Piccadilly Place and turn right along Piccadilly. Take the second right, Albany Courtyard, and stop outside. Built in 1770 for the first Viscount Melbourne and originally called Melbourne House, this building was converted into chambers for bachelors in 1802. Among those who have since lived here are the writers J.B. Priestley, Graham Greene and Aldous Huxley, the politician Sir Edward Heath, the actor Terence Stamp and the poet Lord Byron.

Return along Piccadilly, and pass Burlington House on the right. It is now home to the Royal Academy, and if time allows is well worth a visit. The next building is Burlington Arcade, which was built in 1819 for the owner of Burlington House, Lord George Cavendish. It is said that his lordship built it to stop passers-by throwing their oyster shells and other rubbish into his garden.

As you explore this splendid survivor of Regency London, beware the top-hatted beadle, entrusted with the task of enforcing the arcade's Regency laws that still forbid shoppers to sing, whistle or hurry. Beware also the activities of 'Percy' the poltergeist who in the late 1970s was making a decided nuisance of himself at a leather-goods shop. Some inexplicable happenings included objects being lifted from the shelves in the middle of the night and arranged in neat semi-circles upon the floor. Scotland Yard detectives found themselves at a loss to explain the phenomenon. There was never any sign of a broken entry, nothing was ever missing and there was no damage. After four months the activity ceased as abruptly as it had begun, and it has never been repeated since.

A Strange Meeting Outside Fortnum and Mason

Go back along Piccadilly and cross over at the traffic lights outside the Royal Academy to pause by Fortnum and Mason. Founded in 1707, this upmarket grocery store supplies provisions to the Royal Household.

It was outside the main entrance that journalist and broadcaster, the late Nancy Spain, had a strange encounter. She was standing on Piccadilly desperate to find a taxi to take her to an important appointment. When a taxi eventually pulled up a red-haired old lady got out, but had considerable difficulty finding the necessary change to pay her fare. Frantic to get to her appointment, Nancy paid the woman's fare herself. The old lady thanked her and hurried into Fortnum and Mason. Nancy settled into the back of the taxi. As they drove along the driver laughed and told her, 'You were caught that time... that was old Lady C. She could buy both of us.' The next day Nancy visited her mother and told her what had happened. Her mother looked surprised, picked up a newspaper dated three days earlier and passed it to Nancy. She read, open-mouthed, the headline: 'LADY C. DIES IN FIRE'.

Walk along Duke Street St James's to the right of the store and turn first left into Jermyn Street, which is lined with elegant old-fashioned shops. Floris, the perfumiers, has traded at number 89 since 1810. A little further along on the left is St James's Church, the architect Sir Christopher Wren's only London church to be built on an entirely new site. In 1708 he wrote proudly of it, 'I think it may be found beautiful and convenient.'

Opposite the church, turn right into Duke of York Street and walk its length to arrive in St James's Square. At the centre can be seen an equestrian statue of William III. He sits astride Sorrell, the horse that in 1702 stumbled over a mole-hill and threw him to an ignoble death. The grateful Jacobites marked the anniversary for many years by toasting the 'little gentleman in black velvet' – i.e, the mole responsible for the hill. The statue shows the horse's head as it begins to skew right, capturing the fall as it begins to happen. The molehill can be seen under the horse's left rear leg.

The Ethereal Turn at the Theatre Royal, Haymarket

Go clockwise around the square and exit onto Charles II Street. Cross Waterloo Place and continue walking to arrive at Haymarket. The graceful and attractive theatre was built here in 1821 by John Nash, but saw its greatest success in 1853–78 under the management of J.B. Buckstone, a popular and well known man of the theatre who dedicated almost thirty years of his life to the Haymarket. He died in 1879 and, within a year, his ghost was seen seated in the Royal Box watching a performance.

Since then, many illustrious folk of the theatrical world have seen his spectral form, among them Donald Sinden, who saw him when playing in *The Heiress* with Ralph Richardson in 1949. As he passed Richardson's dressing room, Sinden noticed a man in a long black coat, his back to him, looking out of the window. Thinking it was his co-star he said, 'Goodnight, Ralph,' and continued on his way. It was then he heard a familiar voice and realised that Richardson was still on stage – and so could not have been in his dressing room.

On other occasions stagehands walking past Buckstone's dressing room have quite clearly heard a voice rehearsing lines but, on opening the door, have found the room empty. In 1996 the theatre launched a backstage tour and a group of VIP guests was invited to join a dress rehearsal of the proposed tour. An important inclusion was to be a visit to Buckstone's room, where participants would be treated to anecdotes about the man who had done so much to bring success to the theatre. As the dry run began the stage manager unlocked the dressing-room door and went off to attend to other business. When the party arrived at Buckstone's room, the guide turned the handle and found the door locked. The mystified stage manager returned with the key and attempted to unlock it. No matter how hard he tried, the door remained locked fast and the key just would not work.

From the theatre, go right along Haymarket, then turn left to walk to Piccadilly Circus Underground Station, where the walk ends.

Royal London

Start	St James's Park Underground Station (Circle and District lines)
Finish	Green Park Underground Station (Jubilee, Piccadilly and Victoria lines)
Distance	3 miles (4.8 kilometres)
Duration	2 hours.
Best Time	At night, when much of the route is deserted and the gaslamps lend a delightfully eerie quality to Green Park
Refreshments	The very quaint Sedan Chair pub in Queen Anne's Gate, the Golden Lion in St James's and several pubs, restaurants and cafés in Shepherd's Market towards the end of the walk.

This walk goes through an area with a decidedly royal feel. It includes a refreshing stroll through the delightful St James's Park, where you can admire the abundant and varied species of waterfowl, descendants of those introduced by Charles II. You may also encounter the headless woman who has been known to disturb the peaceful tranquillity of the park from time to time. Then, after passing two Royal Palaces (both haunted), you enter the timeless village of St James's, where several old houses are still visited by residents who have long since shuffled off this mortal coil. The walk ends in the elegant streets of Mayfair. Here is the most haunted house in London, where you might just glimpse the thing that has caused several people to throw themselves to painful deaths from upper windows. The last section, although lacking in ghosts, takes you into the narrow alleyways and courtyards of Shepherd's Market, where you should explore the old-fashioned labyrinth of streets.

Leave St James's Park Underground Station from the Petty France exit and go over the pedestrian crossing into Queen Anne's Gate. Follow it as it turns right and, halfway along, pause by the statue of Queen Anne (1665–1714). There is a local tradition that, at the stroke of midnight on 1 August (the anniversary of the Queen's death), the statue climbs down from the pedestal and walks up and down the street three times. No doubt, as the Queen keeps her annual vigil, she pauses to admire what is architecturally one of the finest streets in London.

Down Cockpit Steps to Meet a Headless Woman

At the end of Queen Anne's Gate go left into Dartmouth Street and then straight ahead to the clearly visible Cockpit Steps. From the bottom of the steps a headless lady is often seen moving across the pavement and drifting over the road in the direction of St James's Park, opposite. *The Times,* told in January 1804, of two Coldstream Guards who were so frightened by her that they were confined to hospital, where they remained seriously ill for some considerable time. In 1972, a motorist driving along here late at night collided with a lamppost when he swerved to avoid a woman in a red dress who suddenly appeared before him. Amazingly, the history of the mysterious haunting was brought up at the subsequent court case and the motorist was acquitted of dangerous driving!

Turn left off the steps and cross the pedestrian crossing into St James's Park, originally laid out for James I in 1603 and re-landscaped for Charles II in 1660. In 1667 he introduced exotic birds to the park. Go along the path through the beautiful and picturesque park and pause on the bridge. This crosses the delightful lake, which dates from 1827, when John Nash re-landscaped the entire park.

A headless woman is sometimes seen in this vicinity. She rises slowly from the dark rippling waters and drifts slowly across the surface of the lake. Reaching dry land, she breaks into a frenzied run, her arms flailing wildly about her. Petrified onlookers stand rooted to the spot as the headless figure rushes towards the bushes and vanishes. In life, she is thought to have been the wife of a sergeant in the guard who murdered her in the 1780s. Having hacked off her head, he buried it in a secret location before flinging her body into the lake, which was then little more than an expanse of marshy ground. Since that fateful day her headless spectre searches in vain for its missing head.

The Spook of Clarence House

Cross the bridge, where you have a superb view of Buckingham Palace on the left. Walk ahead along the path that leads to the Mall and go over the pedestrian crossing, then turn left along the Mall and turn first right into Stable Yard Road. Look through the gates at the house. Built in 1825 for the Duke of Clarence, who was later to become King William IV, Clarence House today is the London home of Her Majesty the Queen Mother. During World War II, the building housed the offices of the Foreign Relations Department of the British Red Cross Society.

In her book *Haunted Royal Homes* Joan Forman tells of a clerk, Sonia Marsh, who was working alone in the vast building one Saturday afternoon when she got the uneasy feeling that something was watching her. Looking into the darkness, she saw a greyish, smoky, triangular mass coming towards her in a bobbing motion. Petrified, she leapt to her feet, grabbed her coat and raced from the building into the chill of a gloomy October afternoon. When on Monday morning she told a colleague of her experience, the woman commented, 'It was probably the Old Duke of Connaught.' Arthur, Duke of Connaught, the third son of Queen Victoria, lived at Clarence House from 1900 until his death in 1942. It would appear, however, that his ghost was roaming the corridors and rooms of his London home for several years afterwards.

Remorse and Suicide at Buckingham Palace

Return to the Mall and pause by the next right turning. You can either cross over or remain here and look at Buckingham Palace. This, the Queen's London residence, was built in 1703 for John Sheffield, the first Duke of Buckingham. George III was the first monarch to own it, beginning a restoration that would con-

ROYAL LONDON

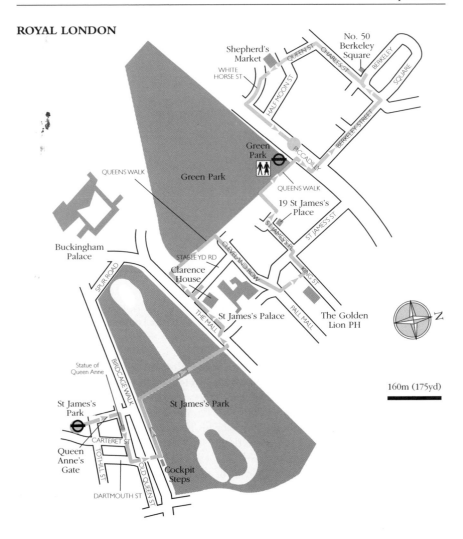

tinue through the reigns of George IV and William IV before the young Queen Victoria moved into the building in 1837.

Long before, a priory once stood here on what was then an inhospitable site surrounded by marshland. Some say that it is the ghost of a monk who died in the monastery's punishment cell that haunts Buckingham Palace. He always appears on Christmas Day, on the terrace overlooking the gardens to the rear of the building. Bound in heavy chains and dressed in brown, he clanks and moans his way backwards and forwards for a few minutes before fading into nothingness, not to be seen again until the next Christmas.

The palace has a second and more contemporary ghost, dating from the reign of Edward VII. Major John Gwynne, the King's private secretary, was involved in a scandalous divorce that meant he was shunned by polite society. In shame, he retired one night to his first-floor office with a revolver and blew out his brains. Since that day, staff working in the vicinity have occasionally heard a gun firing in the room where the suicide occurred.

Green Park's 'Tree of Death'

Turn right along the pathway that goes alongside the park, which is reputed to have been the burial ground for the nearby leper's hospital of St James's. This is said to be the reason for its lack of flowers. Park-keepers whisper in hushed tones about a particular tree which they have dubbed, poetically the 'Tree of Death'. They give it a wide berth when working in the park, no birds sing from its branches, and dogs avoid it. A general feeling of melancholy is said to emanate from it, which may account for the high number of suicides that have been found hanging from its branches. A few witnesses have been scared witless by a throaty, gurgling chuckle that suddenly sounds from inside the tree. Others have caught glimpses of a tall, shadowy figure that stands beside the tree, pointing at them, but which vanishes the moment any brave or curious person moves towards it.

Some way up on the right, go through the gates that lead into the narrow Milkmaid's Passage, named for the days when this was a rural area and maids would come along carrying fresh milk to the dairy of nearby St James's Palace.

St James's Palace and a Cut Throat

Leave the passage and turn onto Cleveland Row. Keep straight ahead to St James's Street, passing the palace on your right. Built by Henry VIII on the site of St James's Hospital for Leprous Women, the Palace was the scene of a particularly grisly event on 31 May, 1810. Ernest Augustus, Duke of Cumberland, was woken in the early hours of that morning by two light blows to his head. As he climbed from his bed to investigate, he was slashed across the thigh by a sabre and fell to the ground crying to his valet, 'Neale, I am murdered.' The wound, however, was not serious and Neale tended it as best he could, then went to fetch the duke's other valet, Sellis. To his horror, he found Sellis lying on his bed with his head virtually cut from his body and a bloody razor in his lifeless hand. The subsequent inquest ruled that Sellis had, for reasons unknown, attacked his master and, in remorse, had committed suicide. Court gossip, however, whispered that the duke had seduced Sellis's daughter and that, when confronted by his valet, the duke had responded by murdering Sellis in a fit of rage. On occasion, when the old palace settles at night and the daytime populace have retired to their beds, the ghost of Sellis walks its corridors and rooms, a gaping wound across his throat, and the sickly, sweet smell of fresh blood trailing in his wake.

Cross over the two pedestrian crossings opposite the main gate of the palace and walk along Pall Mall to turn left into the second alleyway, which is Angel Court. This dark, forbidding passageway, probably named after an ancient inn that once stood here, rises gradually upward to bring you to the Golden Lion, a palatial pub where a ghost of unknown gender is regularly glimpsed in the upstairs bar. Staff clearing up here at night cross to the stairs when, from the corner of their eyes, they glimpse someone at the table to the right of the window. When they turn and look there is nobody there. Customers, too, have seen the ghost from the corner of their eyes, never clearly, and when they look directly at the table it is empty.

Leave the pub and go left along King Street (keeping to the right pavement), cross St James's St by the pedestrian crossing and go straight ahead into St James's Place. A plaque on the wall of number 28 commemorates the statesman William Huskisson (1770–1830), the first person to be run over by a steam train. The large, stately building next door is Spencer House, former ancestral home of the late Diana, Princess of Wales. Follow the road as it bends and, at the very top, go into the almost concealed courtyard on the right.

No. 19 St James's Place – Where Death's Herald Came

The dilapidated, yellow building you are standing outside was, for many years of the last century, the home of two spinster sisters, Ann and Harriet Pearson, who were deeply devoted to each other. After Ann died, in 1858, Harriet lived in the house alone. But in November 1864, while on a visit to Brighton, she fell seriously ill. She was brought back to her London home and nursed by her two nieces, Mrs Coppinger and Miss Emma Pearson, and her nephew's wife, Mrs John Pearson. On 23 December heavy snow began to fall in the street outside, and a thick mist swirled around the windows of the house. Mrs Coppinger and Miss Pearson retired to bed, leaving Mrs Pearson to look after their ailing aunt. They left their door open and the landing gaslight burning. At about one in the morning both jerked awake and saw their dead Aunt Ann go past their open door and into the sick room. Mrs Pearson then rushed into their room in a state of great agitation, having also seen and recognised the dead woman. All three returned to their aunt's bedside, where she told them that she had just seen her sister and knew Ann had come to call her away.

Shortly afterwards, Aunt Harriet slipped into a coma, dying peacefully at 6 o'clock that evening.

No. 50 Berkeley Square – The Most Haunted House in London

Leave the alleyway and take the passageway, to the left of Castlemaine House, that leads back onto Queen's Walk. Turn right, walk to the gates and go right along Piccadilly. Cross over at the traffic lights outside the Ritz Hotel and walk ahead into Berkeley Street. Follow its entire length, then go left and walk clockwise around Berkeley Square. Having passed over the two crossings, you arrive on the left at Maggs Bros situated at number 50.

A century ago this sturdy-looking building had the reputation of being the most haunted house in London. Passers-by were startled by strange lights that flashed in the windows, disembodied screams that sounded from the depths of the building and the still spookier bumping sound of a heavy body being dragged down the staircase. On one occasion a maidservant, newly arrived at the house, was given an upstairs room and duly retired to bed. Two hours later the family were woken by her terrified screams and, racing to her assistance, found her standing in the centre of the room, as rigid as a corpse and with her eyes wide and staring. She was never able to tell what she had seen, for she never regained her sanity. Soon afterwards a young man boasted that he would spend a night in that room. He retired to bed having arranged with the rest of the household that, should he require assistance, he would ring the bell twice. No sooner had he gone to the room than the bell began to ring furiously. When his friends raced upstairs they found him dead, his face twisted and contorted with terror, his open eyes bulging from their sockets.

After this the house became empty and neglected. Then one day two sailors who had enjoyed a night on the town broke in and made their way to an upper room, where they lay down to sleep. They were woken by the sound of heavy, determined footsteps coming up the stairs. Suddenly the door banged open and a hideous, shapeless, oozing mass began to fill the room. One sailor managed to get past it and escape. Returning to the house with a policeman, he found his comrade's mutilated corpse impaled on the railings. The twisted face and bulging eyes were grim testimony to the terror that had caused the man to jump to his death.

Today the building seems peacefully at odds with its traumatic past, and Maggs Bros, who have traded here for close on forty years, sneer at suggestions that their premises are haunted by a hideous entity. But some say that the house still gives off a strange and creepy aura, and it has been claimed that the building is so charged with psychic energy that merely touching the exterior brickwork sends a shiver down the spine and a cold chill to the marrow of the psychically inclined.

Go back to the crossing and turn right into Charles Street, turning first left into Queen Street, Mayfair. Go over the two crossings, turn left into Curzon Street and then right through the covered passage into Shepherd's Market. This charming network of narrow streets and alleys was laid out in 1735 on the site of the May Fair that gave the area its name. Pass the Grapes pub and continue ahead into Whitehorse Street, a gloomy thoroughfare that leads to Piccadilly. Turn left and walk to Green Park Underground Station, where the walk ends.

Belgravia and Chelsea

Location   2–3 miles (3.2–4.8 kilometres) west of Charing Cross.
Refreshments   The Grenadier Pub featured in this chapter. Numerous bars and cafés on the King's Road.

The walks in this chapter are broken down into short visits, although it is quite possible to enjoy a pleasant stroll through these two districts that would last about two hours. You could begin by walking through the exquisite, though uniform, streets of Belgravia before crossing the border into Chelsea, renowned for its Bohemian residents, both past and present.

Belgravia was developed by the builder Thomas Cubitt (1788–1855) in the 1820s on a flat, treeless expanse known as the Five Fields. Owned by the Grosvenor family, Belgravia is named for their Leicestershire estate, Belgrave and is now considered London's most exclusive residential neighbourhood. Number 33 Belgrave Square is the home of the Spiritualist Society, and members of the public can attend regular public demonstrations by mediums or have a private sitting by appointment.

Chelsea, on the other hand, has long had a reputation as a Bohemian quarter, and its streets and houses are as varied as the residents who have lived here. In picturesque sidestreets you come across blue plaques declaring that residents such as Bram Stoker, Mark Twain and Oscar Wilde lived here. The Royal Hospital, home to the fabled Chelsea Pensioners, is open to the public at certain times and is a delight to discover.

To best enjoy these villages I recommend you take with you Andrew Duncan's *Walking London* (new edition, 1999) and slot the haunted places into the narrative.

1. Cromwell's Ghost at Apsley House

Nearest Underground Station: Hyde Park Corner (Piccadilly Line)

After victory over Napoleon's forces at the Battle of Waterloo, Arthur Wellesley, Duke of Wellington, became a national hero. However, when he was the Tory Prime Minister, he vehemently opposed the Reform Bill of 1832 and found himself the most unpopular man in the land. On more than one occasion, the 'Iron Duke' was besieged by an angry mob at his home, Apsley House. Among the exhibits of his personal memorabilia, on show at what is now the Wellington Museum, is a dagger-tipped umbrella that he carried for his personal protection. Matters came to a head in 1832 when the Lords refused point-blank to give the Reform Bill passage through Parliament. The London mob mobilised and it looked as though a revolution was imminent. But inexplicably the Duke of Wellington suddenly changed his mind, gave his support to the Bill, and persuaded the Lords to pass it. It would be many years before the bizarre reason for Wellington's change of heart would be made public.

It was a ghostly visitation that brought it about – the ghost being that of Oliver Cromwell. One night, as the mob outside bayed for his blood, Wellington was on his way to bed. As the light from his candle flickered, the figure of Cromwell suddenly came at him from the shadows of a corridor. With a reproachful gaze, the ghost turned slowly towards the window, stretched out an arm, uncurled a finger and pointed in the direction of the howling mob. Turning back to the duke, the apparition waved a finger in admonishment and vanished. Wellington deduced that Cromwell had come to warn him to relinquish his opposition to the Reform Bill, which he duly did, and it finally passed smoothly through Parliament in June 1832.

2. The Grenadier Public House, Wilton Row
Nearest Underground Station: Hyde Park Corner (Piccadilly Line)
Wilton Mews is a delightful, hidden nook a few minutes away from the bustle of Hyde Park Corner, yet it has a sleepy village atmosphere. Colourful mews cottages line the cobblestones, and nestling within this tranquil serenity is one of London's most enchanting pubs, the Grenadier, reputed to have once been the officers' mess of a near-by barracks. The cellars were a drinking and gambling lair for the common soldiers.

Here a young subaltern, caught cheating at cards, was beaten and flogged so severely by his fellow players that he died from his injuries. His death is thought to have occurred in September, for this is the month when the pub experiences an onslaught of ghostly activity. A solemn, silent figure moves slowly through the tiny, low-ceilinged rooms. Objects shift mysteriously in the night, tables and chairs are rattled by an unseen hand, and a strange icy chill hangs in the air and has sent a marrow-chilling shiver down the backs of many customers. Footsteps are heard pacing around empty rooms and, very occasionally, a low sighing moan emanates from the cellar. On one occasion a Chief Superintendent from New Scotland Yard was enjoying a drink in the pub when wisps of smoke began to waft around him. His curiosity aroused, he reached towards what he took to be the source of the smoke and pulled his hand back in agony as it was burnt by an unseen cigarette.

The combination of haunting, history and timelessness makes the Grenadier one of the most alluring pubs in the neighbourhood, and a visit, whether rewarded by a ghostly appearance or not, is well worth the effort.

3. Eaton Place's Drowned Admiral
Nearest Underground Station: Sloane Square (Circle and District lines)
On 22 June, 1893, Admiral Sir George Tryon was on manoeuvres with the Mediterranean Fleet off the coast of Syria. Suddenly he gave orders for his ship, the *Victoria,* and the nearby *Camperdown* to turn inwards and steam towards each other. It was obvious to all on board that the manoeuvre could lead only to disaster, but none of his subordinates dared question or overrule the extraordinary order and, in consequence, the two ships collided and the *Victoria* sank. As the ship went down, taking four hundred men and the admiral himself to a watery grave, Tryon was heard to say, 'It is entirely my fault.'

Plate 10: *When the resident ghost starts making its presence felt, a visit to the Flask tavern in Highgate can be a chilling experience for the psychically inclined (see page 43).*

Plate 11: *With its decaying mausoleums and tangled creepers the Western section of Highgate Cemetery abounds in atmosphere and ghostly and vampiric activity (see page 44).*

Plates 12 and 13: *Highwayman Dick Turpin. Previous pages: accidentally shooting his best friend. Above: Hampstead Heath, where his shade gallops towards unsuspecting walkers (see page 52).*

Plate 14: *Burlington Arcade, home in the 1970s to 'Percy' the poltergeist (see page 62).*

Plate 15: *Theatre Royal's Victorian Manager has been seen by many famous actors (see page 63).*

BELGRAVIA AND CHELSEA

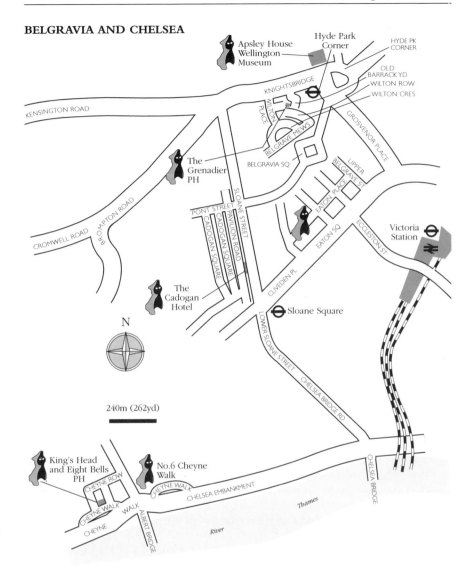

At the exact moment that Tryon was plummeting to the ocean bed, his wife was holding an At Home at their house in Eaton Place. Suddenly Sir George, resplendent in full regalia, appeared before over a hundred guests, strolled across the room, then turned and vanished. Lady Tryon did not herself see him, and was mystified when told that her husband had just walked through the room. She explained to the bemused guests that he was far away at sea. It was the next day before news of the tragedy reached England and Lady Tryon realised that what the guests had seen was her husband's ghost.

4. Lillie Langtry Walks the Cadogan Hotel

Nearest Underground Station: Sloane Square (Circle and District lines)

The Cadogan Hotel is where Oscar Wilde stayed to await his inevitable arrest after losing his libel action against the Marquis of Queensberry. The hotel was also home to Lillie Langtry, the 'Jersey Lily', mistress to the Prince of Wales, Bertie, the future Edward VII. Lillie's ghost haunts the private dining rooms, which now occupy her former living quarters. She seems to be a shy and unassuming spectre who appears only at quiet periods, such as on Christmas Day, when the hotel is largely empty.

5. George Eliot's Death and No. 4, Cheyne Walk

Nearest Underground Station: Sloane Square (Circle and District lines)

A charming cluster of Georgian houses line this terrace, which is set a little way back from the river. Its list of residents, past and present, is perhaps more distinguished than anywhere else in Chelsea. A plaque on the wall of number 4 commemorates Mary Ann Evans (1819–1880), better known as novelist George Eliot, who moved here on 3 December, 1880, and died nineteen days later from a chill. The writer Katharine Macqoid had intended to visit Eliot, but had not found the time to do so. Then, early one morning, she woke from a troubled sleep to see the novelist standing at the bottom of her bed. She heard a voice murmur the number 'sixty-one', and took it as a prophecy that she would die at that age. But the meaning became tragically clear when, later that day, her son rushed round to tell her that George Eliot had died in the night at the age of sixty-one.

6. The Misogynist of King's Head and Eight Bells

Nearest Underground Station: Sloane Square (Circle and District lines)

Towards the end of Cheyne Walk, as it reaches Chelsea Old Church, there is a high-class restaurant that was formerly a pub known as the King's Head and Eight Bells. As a pub it was a favoured haunt of writers, artists and rock stars, including Ian Fleming and various members of the Rolling Stones.

As a pub, it had its origins in the days when Chelsea was an isolated rural village. It was haunted by an unseen entity that became particularly active when a new female member of staff came to work there. The landlady would often come down in the morning to find that glasses have been rearranged and objects such as the till keys had been moved about.

In October 1997 the ghost's impish penchant for mischief-making took a dangerous twist. The landlady's husband was working in the cellar one morning when he thought he heard running water in a back storeroom. Going to investigate, he discovered that three gas cylinders, delivered seven days earlier, were turned full on. Later in 1997, during the weekend before Christmas, a new barmaid started at the pub, and the ghost reacted by constantly switching off the central heating.

Kensington to
Notting Hill

Location   3 miles (4.8 kilometres) north-west of Charing Cross.
Refreshments Various pubs and cafés on Kensington High Street.

Until the 19th century, Kensington was an independent village outside the limits of London. That changed when, in 1689, William III acquired the home of the Earl of Nottingham and made it into his palace at Kensington. It soon became the residence of the reigning monarch and would remain so until the death of George II there in 1760. Around the palace, the village of Kensington developed to accommodate those who needed or wished to be near the palace, and today it is a delightful area of quiet Georgian squares, village streets and mews (formerly stable yards). When William was settling into the palace, Knightsbridge was nothing more than a sleepy hamlet, named for a bridge over the river Westbourne where legend holds that two knights duelled to the death. But Knightsbridge too, was soon swallowed up as polite society moved westwards and today, like its neighbour, Kensington, it is a smart and fashionable area.

The hauntings in the areas are too spread out to make a cohesive walk so I have listed the places where ghosts have been seen and numbered them on the accompanying map.

1. The Face-Puller of Lowndes Square
Nearest Underground Station: Knightsbridge (Piccadilly line)
Lowndes Square has always been considered a smart address, and at least one former resident seems to be so attracted to it that she returns in spectral form to sit and gaze at the splendid houses. Several people have reported seeing a white-haired old woman in an old-fashioned bath chair that sits at the kerb. She pulls the most terrible faces whenever they look at her. It is reputed to be the ghost of an old woman who had suffered a stroke and was brought by her daughter to live with her at her house in the square. On sunny days the daughter would place her mother in the bath chair and sit her outside in the street where, whenever she became bored, the stroke having deprived her of her speech, she would make grotesque faces at passers-by in the hope that someone would ring the bell of her daughter's house so that she could be taken back inside.

2. Montpelier Square and a Perturbed Wife
Nearest Underground Station: Knightsbridge (Piccadilly Line)
An interesting tale of a single haunting where a ghost appears to save the soul of

a living relative is told in Charles Harper's *Haunted Houses* concerns an unidentified house in Montpelier Square. In December 1913 a clergyman leaving his nearby church was approached by a lady in a considerable state of agitation. She told him that a dying man who lived nearby was worried about the state of his soul and wished to consult a man of God. The vicar went with her to a waiting cab, and they were taken the short distance to an imposing town house in Montpelier Square. The vicar knocked on the door and was answered by a butler, who confirmed that the man whom the lady had named did live there. He added that the man was in perfect health. Turning for an explanation, the clergyman was astonished to find that both the lady and the cab had disappeared from sight. Moments later the owner of the house came down and invited the vicar to come inside. He told him: 'It is very strange… that you should be sent on such an errand in such a mysterious way… I have been troubled lately about the state of my soul, and I have been seriously contemplating calling on you to discuss the matter.'

The clergyman stayed for about an hour, listening to the man's confession. As he left it was agreed that the man would begin afresh the next day by attending the church service, after which they would continue with their discussion.

When the man failed to appear at the church, the vicar returned to the house to see what had happened. He was met again by the butler, to be told that the master of the house had died the previous evening. The butler led him upstairs to the room where the man's body lay, and the clergyman saw on the table a portrait of the lady who had first brought him to the house. 'Who is this?' he asked. 'That,' came the reply, 'is my master's wife, who died fifteen years ago.'

3. Kensington Palace

Nearest Underground Station: High Street Kensington (Circle and District lines)
It is said that a feeling of melancholy hangs over Kensington Palace, and many who have lived here certainly seem to have succumbed to its air of desolation and despair. It first became a Royal Palace during the reign of William III, and later, George II died here. His last days were spent anxiously awaiting the arrival of long overdue dispatches from his beloved Hanover. He would glance up at the weather vane that stood over the entrance, watching for the wind to change direction and speed his messengers to him. His courtiers would hear his sorrowful voice, muttering in broken English, 'Vy dondt dey com?' When the dispatches did finally arrive it was too late; the King had died a short time before. Now, his ghostly face appears at the window of his chambers. Fretful and careworn, he still stares wide-eyed at the palace weather vane. From time to time, his ethereal voice echoes through the chambers, repeating over and over again the question that preoccupied his last days: 'Vy dondt dey com?'

During the reign of George III, several members of the royal family lived at Kensington Palace, among them the King's fifth daughter, the Princess Sophia. The princess fell deeply in love with a royal equerry, Thomas Garth, by whom she had an illegitimate son. With the birth of the child, Garth's ardour diminished and poor Sophia retreated to a lonely existence in her apartments in Kensington Palace. As

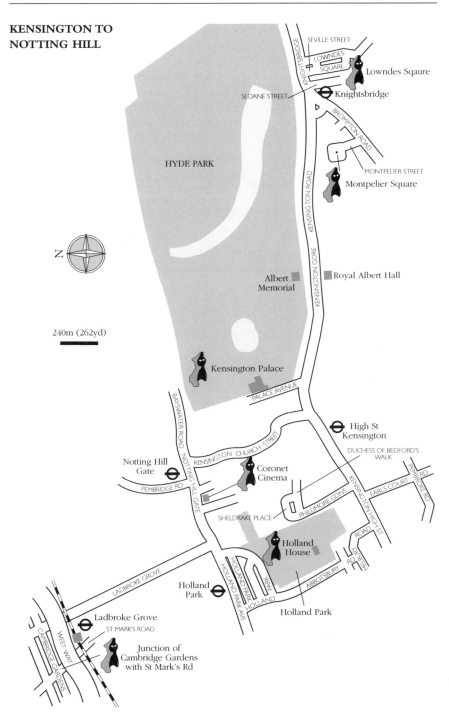

KENSINGTON TO NOTTING HILL

SEVILLE STREET

KNIGHTSBRIDGE

LOWNDES SQUARE

Lowndes Sqaure

SLOANE STREET

Knightsbridge

BROMPTON ROAD

HYDE PARK

KENSINGTON ROAD

MONTPELIER STREET

Montpelier Square

N

KENSINGTON GORE

Albert Memorial

Royal Albert Hall

240m (262yd)

Kensington Palace

PALACE AVENUE

High St Kensington

BAYSWATER ROAD

DUCHESS OF BEDFORD'S WALK

Notting Hill Gate

NOTTING HILL GATE

KENSINGTON CHURCH STREET

Coronet Cinema

PEMBRIDGE RD

PEMBROKE RD

EARLS COURT

PHILLIMORE GDNS

KENSINGTON HIGH ST

SHELDRAKE PLACE

Holland House

Holland Park

HOLLAND PARK

HOLLAND PARK AVE

PARK

ABBOTSBURY

MELBURY RD

LADBROKE GROVE

Holland Park

Ladbroke Grove

ST MARK'S ROAD

Holland Park

WEST WAY

CAMBRIDGE GARDENS

Junction of Cambridge Gardens with St Mark's Rd

time passed, and old age crept upon her, her eyesight began to fail, and she became a sad, pathetic figure whose only solace was to sit at her spinning wheel or to toil at her embroidery frame. Tragically, even this diversion became impossible when her sight failed. She was moved to nearby York House and there she lived out the remainder of her days. Her spirit often returns to the rooms at Kensington Palace where she suffered so much unhappiness. The sound of her ghostly spinning wheel, cranked by her unseen spectral form, has often disturbed the night-time peace, its squeaking, creaking rhythmic sound reverberating through the palace as the hours of darkness slip slowly by.

4. The Headless Earl of Holland House.
Nearest Underground Station: Holland Park (Central Line).
Although devastated by the bombing of World War II, enough of the frontage survives to remind us of what a fairytale palace Holland House once was. Its gables and oriel windows, diminutive stone towers and exquisite arched colonnades sit uneasily alongside its modern neighbour, the Commonwealth Institute. It was built in 1606 for Sir Walter Cope, Chancellor of the Exchequer to James I. He left it to his wife in his will, on condition she did not remarry. When she did, the house passed to their daughter, Lady Rich, whose husband was created Earl of Holland in 1624 and beheaded for his royalist sympathies at the end of the Civil War. It was his ghost that haunted Holland House, and he still pays occasional visits to the youth hostel that now occupies the surviving house's wing. His manifestations were always preceded by three drops of blood that appeared, mysteriously, alongside a hidden door. Then, as the clock struck midnight, his spectre would emerge from a hidden recess and, head tucked under his arm, drift slowly through the rooms and along the corridors of his old home.

5. Cambridge Gardens and a Spectral Bus
Nearest Underground Station: Ladbroke Grove (Hammersmith & City Line)
At its junction with St Mark's Road, Cambridge Gardens is haunted by what must surely be one of the strangest ghosts encountered thus far, a number 7 double-decker ghost bus, last seen in May 1990.

In 1934 a motorist driving along Cambridge Gardens in the early hours of the morning suddenly swerved, crashed into a lamppost and died when his car burst into flames. At the subsequent inquest many witnesses testified to the existence of a phantom bus that often appeared at the spot where the crash had occurred. It would come racing along the centre of the road towards them, forcing them to swerve to avoid a collision. Yet, as they sat shaking at the side of road, they would look back to find the bus had vanished.

After the inquest, others came forward to report their own strange experiences with the ghostly bus. Most agreed that the bus always appeared at more or less the same time, 1.15am. It was always a number 7, no driver was ever visible and no lights were ever on. It was quite distinctive in appearance as it thundered toward astonished onlookers, but the moment it had driven by and they turned to look it had disappeared without trace.

6. The Unquiet Cashier of the Coronet Cinema

Nearest Underground Station: Notting Hill Gate (Central, Circle and District lines)

Boasting one of London's most glorious cinema interiors, the Coronet began as the Coronet Theatre and has since resisted attempts to change its use. A furious preservation battle was waged and won and the Coronet now stands, battered by time, its beautiful Art Nouveau interior strangely at odds with the Hollywood blockbusters that flicker across its screen.

The origins of its ghostly resident go back to the days when the building was a successful theatre and the takings at the box office were quite considerable. One Christmas in the early 1900s a cashier was caught stealing from the till and, confronted by the manager, rushed from his office, ran up to the Gods and threw herself from the balcony. Thereafter, when staff meetings were held in the upper section of the cinema her ghost caused so much disturbance that such meetings were transferred to offices lower down in the building. Footsteps have often been heard climbing the stairs that lead to the Gods, and on one occasion pots of paint were moved by an unseen hand from a room that was awaiting decoration. Staff have more or less come to accept the inconvenience that their resident spectre causes. The ghost is most active in Christmas week, the anniversary of the cashier's suicide.

Chiswick

Start	Turnham Green Underground Station (District and Piccadilly lines)
Finish	Stamford Brook Underground Station (District Line)
Distance	4 miles (6.4 kilometres)
Duration	2 hours
Best Times	Daylight hours, or better still, Twilight in the winter months.
Refreshments	The Tabard Inn at the start of the walk, the Black Lion at the end of the walk, and numerous pubs and fast-food outlets en route.

This walk goes through two distinctive and delightful parts of London, featuring an array of hauntings that includes a mad cook, two of Oliver Cromwell's daughters and a disturbing bout of 20th-century poltergeist activity.

The walk begins in England's first garden suburb, Bedford Park. There follows an uneventful mid-section along Chiswick High Road and across the busy A4 before you arrive amid the tranquil, wooded grounds of the beautiful Chiswick House. The last section of the walk is almost rural in its setting: you amble gently along a picturesque reach of the Thames, lined with grand 17th-and 18th-century houses, to finish at a wonderfully evocative old pub, which has a salutary tale of a haunting that led to tragedy.

The Tabard Inn
Turn right out of the Underground station, go past the line of shops, and walk a little further along to the inn. The Tabard was built in 1880 and designed by the architect Norman Shaw (1831–1912). It became the archetypal English pub, and its style was much imitated by pub builders over the next fifty years. The Tabard is haunted by the shade of an old lady, dressed all in black, who sits at tables saying nothing but apparently whistling to herself, although no sound is ever heard.

Go left out of the pub, cross Bath Road at the crossing, keep straight on into The Avenue and take the first left into Bedford Road. You are now walking through the streets of London's first garden suburb. Bedford Park was created as a middle-class commuting village in the 1880s and soon became a community of writers, artists and other Bohemians. The peaceful streets through which you now stroll are lined with pretty and spacious houses.

The Poltergeist of Esmond Road
Upon arrival at a Victorian pillar box, go left into Esmond Road. A little way along on the right, a line of post-war council houses seem strangely at odds with their larger Victorian neighbours. In July 1956 the inhabitants of one of these houses

became the targets of a poltergeist, who would throw pennies at them. The coins appeared from nowhere and struck several members of the household. Their thirteen-year-old son, David, was struck in the face. When razor blades began to drift around the house and a spanner thrown by an unseen hand smashed a window pane, the family called the police. The two constables sent to investigate were, at first, suspicious of the claims. But, when one of them went to search the garden and was also struck by a flying penny, they became as mystified as the family. Finally, it was decided that whatever was responsible for the phenomenon was focusing on young David and it was decided to send him to stay with relatives for a time. No sooner had he left than the activity ceased and, fortunately, it did not resume upon his return.

Chiswick Police Station

Continue along Esmond Road, turn right onto South Parade and, at the mini-roundabout, go left to pass under the two railway bridges into Fisher's Lane. Turn left onto Chiswick High Road, go over the pedestrian crossing and turn left over Linden Gardens to arrive at the police station. This squat modern building stands on the site of Linden House, an 18th-century manor where, in 1792, a Mrs Abercrombie was hacked to death by her son-in-law, Thomas Wainwright. In the 1950s Chiswick Fire Station occupied the site, and firemen would frequently hear the sounds of a woman's footsteps walking briskly around the basement during the early hours of the morning. The noises would always stop the moment anyone opened the basement door and switched on the lights. Since the building became Chiswick Police Station the basement has been devoid of ghostly activity, although a spectral lady has been known to put in ghostly appearances on the third floor of the new building.

Backtrack over Linden Gardens to walk along narrow Linden Passage, opposite. This later changes to Bourne Passage and, having crossed Duke's Avenue, becomes Barley Mow Passage. Go through the latter and keep ahead onto Heathfield Terrace.

Shudders in the Chiswick Warehouse

Just past the post office, on your left, a dominating building with round roof windows towers above you. Built in the 1870s on the site of a former barracks, this imposing construction, the Chiswick Warehouse, has been a West London landmark ever since. Today it offers comfortable and spacious luxury apartments. Twenty years ago it was a storage warehouse, with a second floor that workers were reluctant to visit alone. They whispered of an intense feeling of icy coldness that would suddenly grip those who ventured there. There was talk of a mysterious, sinister-looking man seen lurking in the shadows and of strange shapes that twisted and writhed across the ceilings. One porter was astonished when a little old man appeared from nowhere, walked briskly past him, and disappeared through a solid locked door, while others complained of invisible fingers that poked them hard in the back as they carried out their duties. The building's conversion to luxury flats has apparently stilled whatever restless spirits lurked on the second floor, for none of the residents have complained of anything untoward occurring... yet!

Spectral Breakfast in Chiswick House

Continue along Heathfield Terrace and, after the Town Hall, go left into Sutton Court Road. A long uneventful walk now takes you over the very busy Ellesmere Road (via the pedestrian crossing). Continue along Sutton Court Road and take the second left into Staveley Road and then the third left into Burlington Lane. A little way along, pass through the white gate to enter the grounds of Chiswick House.

CHISWICK

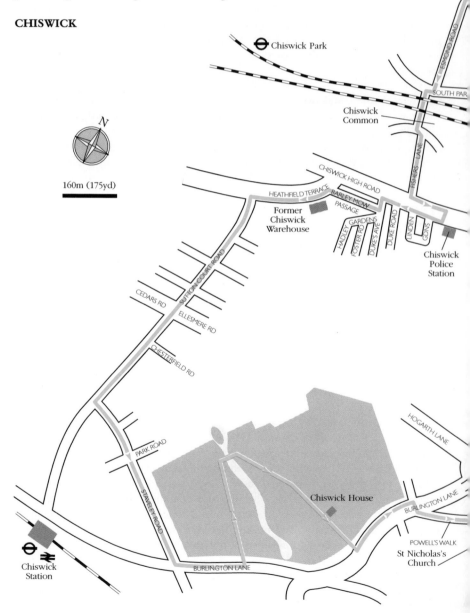

Immediately the mood changes. The uneventful housing that has been your escort for the last ten or so minutes gives way to peaceful, dense woodland. Dark paths wind their way through thick shrubbery and tall majestic trees tower over you. Continue past the obelisk and head toward the white domed building that is visible in the distance. Be warned, for this path, surrounded by skeletal trees and fringed with thick vegetation, can be an unnerving place to wander, even on the

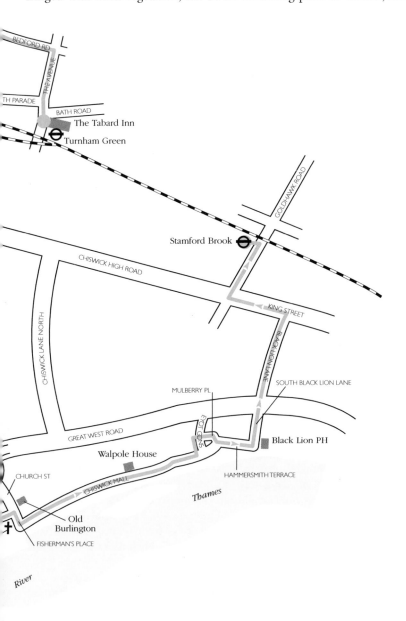

brightest of days. Some say that they catch glimpses of a dark, shadowy figure that moves through the undergrowth, keeping pace with them every step of the way.

Go left off the path, skirt the lake, turn right over the bridge and make your way to the house. It was inspired by the 16th-century Italian architect Andrea Palladio's Villa Capra (or Villa Rotonda) in Vicenza, Italy, and designed by the Earl of Burlington in 1725. Chiswick House was a monument to the earl's appreciation of art, and was used as a meeting place for artists, sculptors and influential politicians before becoming a home and an entertainment venue for various dukes of Devonshire. Two Prime Ministers have died here, Charles James Fox in 1806 and George Canning in 1827. Later in the 19th century it became a lunatic asylum before being abandoned and left to fall into disrepair. It was bought by Middlesex County Council and transferred to the ownership of the Ministry of Works in 1958.

The new occupants set about an extensive restoration project designed to return the building to its original splendour. It was during this refurbishment that the inexplicable smell of bacon and eggs would waft around the building. The workmen laughed it off as the ghost of 'one of the mad cooks'. Ever since, though, staff and visitors have constantly been mystified by the distinctive smell of fried bacon that permeates the back gallery and can hang in the air for up to three months, then not be noticed for a few years. Some visitors claim to sense a female presence in the bedchamber and one lady looking in the mirror there – the only original mirror in the house – was dumbfounded to see the distinctive form of Lady Burlington reflected behind her, but on turning, she found the room empty.

The Haunted Churchyard of St Nicholas

Leave Chiswick House by the main entrance, and go left along Burlington Lane. Cross at the pedestrian crossing, continue left, then turn right into Powell's Walk. As you pass along this narrow pathway, high brick walls rise up on either side. Gradually the noise of the traffic becomes a distant murmur, while the glass and steel that for a moment threatened to engulf you in a tide of urban development give way to a picturesque, almost rural setting. On arrival at the robust green iron gates of a burial ground, follow the path left and make your way to a strikingly handsome stone parish church. Founded in the 15th century, this was dedicated to St Nicholas, the patron saint of sailors and fishermen, when Chiswick was a fishing village. Although the church was rebuilt in 1882, the tower is original and dates from 1446.

Barbara Villiers, whom we shall encounter again at Walpole House, is buried here in an unmarked grave, and the churchyard contains a fine memorial to the engraver William Hogarth. The churchyard is haunted by the white-clad figures of Mary Fauconburg and Frances Rich, daughters of Oliver Cromwell. After their father's death, they lived to a glorious and ripe old age. Rumours have long circulated that, following her father's posthumous beheading (see page 40), Mary bribed a guard to allow her to smuggle her father's headless corpse away from Tyburn, and that she subsequently had it re-interred in the same vault here at St Nicholas's Church where she and her sister would eventually rest.

When the church was rebuilt in 1882 the vicar decided to investigate the rumour and he opened the vault. He found the coffins of the two sisters but also spied a third coffin, which showed signs of rough usage, pushed hard against the wall on the far side of the vault. Fearing the arrival of groups of sightseers to moralise over Cromwell, he had the vault bricked up and left it unmarked. Perhaps the fact that their resting place was desecrated by a vicar who, by his own admission, disliked everything their father stood for is why the two spirits return to wander amongst the graves. They drift through the early morning mists until the first rays of daylight are heralded by the dawn chorus, then melt into the wall of the church and return to their unmarked grave.

Old Burlington's 'Percy'
With your back to the church go a little way along Church Street where, on the right with a large lamp outside, is Old Burlington. The timbered walls of this quaint old house once echoed to the chatter of the tap room and the clink of beer tankards, but the building has long since been converted to a pleasant private house. It is haunted by a good-humoured, harmless old ghost, who sports a wide-brimmed black hat and a billowing cloak. Since he is content just to stare out from the upper windows and cause no inconvenience, he is left to his own devices by residents, who have christened him 'Percy'.

A Lost Beauty in Walpole House
Go back towards the church, keeping to the left pavement. Go down the hill and bear left onto Chiswick Mall. To your right is one of the prettiest and most picturesque urban reaches of the Thames. The Mall is a place to absorb the peaceful ambience of the riverside location as you stroll at a leisurely pace, admiring the splendid houses, which date from between the 17th and 20th centuries. Keep ahead until, some distance along on the left, you arrive at Walpole House.

For the last two years of her life, a famed royal concubine ebbed out her days in this peaceful, modest house overlooking the Thames. The diarist Samuel Pepys called her 'the curse of the nation' yet, when he dreamt of holding her in his arms, he commented that, if death meant slipping into such a dreamlike existence, it wouldn't be too bad! Her name was Barbara Villiers (1640–1709), Duchess of Cleveland; she was mistress of King Charles II and arguably the greatest beauty of 17th-century society. By the time she came to live here, her royal lover had been dead some twenty years and, worse still, her appearance had begun to change alarmingly. She had swelled 'gradually to a monstrous bulk', which her physicians diagnosed as due to dropsy, and her time here proved one of the most miserable periods of her illustrious life. Local residents would whisper of seeing her, bathed in moonlight, standing at the windows, her hands clasped to her breast, imploring her maker to restore her beauty. But her pleas went unanswered, the dropsy proved incurable, and, on Sunday 9 October, 1709, at the age of 67, she breathed her last tortured breath.

But Barbara did not go gently. Although beauty might only be skin deep, for her the lament of its loss was eternal. When the full moon casts its eerie hue upon the Mall, its shimmering light illuminating the windows of her old house, Barbara's puffy, bloated face can still sometimes be seen, pressed against the glass, her dark eyes rolling in despair as she implores and begs for the restoration of her lost looks.

Others have heard the distinctive tap of her high heels moving backwards and forwards across the upper floor as her restless spirit relives time and time again the agonies of those final years at Walpole House.

The Black Lion
Continue along Chiswick Mall, then turn left into Eyot Gardens and first right into Mulberry Place. Follow the right bend to turn left along Hammersmith Terrace, at the end of which is the Black Lion. Two hundred years ago, a piggery stood on the site now occupied by this delightful old pub. The pig farmer began to brew beer for himself and his friends, and this proved so popular that it soon overtook his farming interests and the Black Lion was born.

Black Lion Lane, on which the pub stands, was much troubled from 1804 onwards by the Hammersmith Ghost. This white, shrouded, spectral form would wail, moan and writhe its way around the vicinity causing much terror to local residents. The haunting reached a tragic climax when an excise officer, Francis Smith, 'filled his blunderbuss with shot, and himself with ale' and went out to lay the ghost. Unfortunately he mistakenly shot dead a white-clothed plasterer, Thomas Millwood, who was on his way home from work. The subsequent inquest was held at the pub and full details of that fateful night can be read in a newspaper cutting now displayed inside. The bar staff, working alone in the early morning, have often heard strange, anxious footsteps pacing back and forth across the upper floor. The pub has known other uncanny doings. Towards the rear is the Long Room, an eerie place at the busiest of times. A barmaid happened to glance into it one morning and noticed a pretty little girl, wearing an Alice in Wonderland-style dress, skipping along the centre aisle. Wondering who the child was, she went to investigate and found the room completely empty.

And so the walk draws to its cosy finale. The nearest underground station is Stamford Brook. Reach it by walking along Black Lion Lane, go under the pedestrian subway, continue left at the church and walk to King Street. Turn left and then right at the traffic lights into Goldhawk Road. A little way along on the left is Stamford Brook Underground Station, where the walk ends.

Wimbledon

Location	7½ miles (12 kilometres) southwest of Charing Cross.
Transport	Wimbledon Station (Overground trains from Waterloo Station; Underground District Line)
Refreshments	Many pubs, restaurants and coffee shops on the High Street.

Wimbledon has been one of London's most select suburbs for nigh on two hundred years, though it is perhaps most famous for its international tennis championships. Its 1,045-acre (423-hectares) Common is covered with gorse, bracken and trees and can be extremely desolate and eerie. Haunted sites include the Common, the Wimbledon Theatre and a street that was once renowned as a centre of the Spiritualist movement. Now the venue of much supernatural phenomena, this was the home of one of the 19th century's great investigative journalists, who prophesied his own untimely death in a maritime disaster. The sites are spread out and are numbered in order so they can be followed on the accompanying map.

1. Wimbledon Theatre, Wimbledon Broadway

The theatre opened on 26 December, 1910, with the pantomime *Jack and Jill* and the tradition of family Christmas shows is still going strong. The original manager of the theatre was the impresario J.B. Mulholland, and from time to time his ghostly form has appeared sitting in one of the theatre boxes, content to watch the play being performed or to oversee rehearsals at his beloved theatre.

Far more active is the 'Grey Lady', who in 1980 appeared in the bedroom of the manageress as just a head and torso that proceeded to ascend before the startled lady's gaze and vanished into the ceiling, omitting a raucous cackle as she went. Numerous stage hands and usherettes have seen her misty form, sometimes sitting in the front row of the gallery, at other times passing through closed doors and on one occasion strolling contentedly out of the ladies' toilet.

The ghost also has the annoying habit of switching on the sprinkler system; when this last occurred, staff quickly lowered the safety curtain to prevent the orchestra pit from being flooded. Subsequently the bemused staff members were most surprised to discover that, although the water had got into the orchestra pit, the safety curtain itself had remained completely dry.

2. Hillside – Wimbledon's Most Haunted Street

The ghost of a young girl has been seen walking across several of the gardens. She appears between the hours of 11pm and midnight, is about twelve years old and

WIMBLEDON

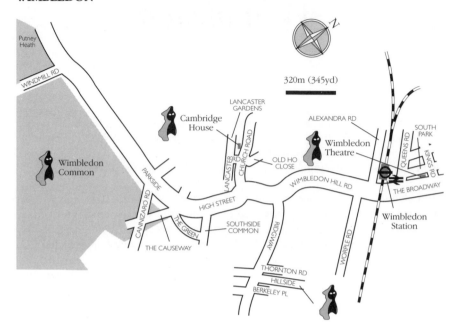

wears a loose-fitting chemise. She is seen walking towards the houses but apparently has second thoughts and turns and fades away as she walks slowly off.

At another house an unseen spirit has the habit of locking visitors in an upstairs room. Try as they might, the unfortunate victims find it impossible to open the door from the inside, although anyone outside the room can open the door with ease. The owner of the house once found herself locked in the dreaded room at night and got a feeling of something so malevolent in the room that she leapt from the window to escape its clutches. People who have parked their cars in the street have come back to find that, although their vehicle is locked and the alarm still on, their possessions have been thrown around the interior by an unseen hand.

It has been observed that any form of psychic activity in a building can disturb the spirits of those who once lived there. From 1934 to 1941, Hillside was associated with a Spiritualist group, the headquarters of which were known as 'The House of Red Cloud'. The group operated under the auspices of the medium Estelle Roberts (1889–1970), whom Maurice Barbanell, a founder of *Psychic News*, described as 'one of the world's greatest mediums and the possessor of nearly every psychic faculty'.

Red Cloud was the Native American who acted as her spirit guide, and, although mostly content to assist the bereaved in contacting their deceased loved ones, he was also able to materialise before sitters. One account of such a manifestation tells how a billowing cloud appeared, that was 'becoming slowly more and more visible as it grew in volume'. Suddenly, it became apparent that a face was appearing before those present, although it swiftly disappeared. Red Cloud then asked for a torch and, once one had been held out, 'the next instant it was high over the heads of the circle, flashing on and off as though being tested'. As the torch moved across the room to where ectoplasm had formed, the 'strong, cleanly etched features of Red Cloud' became visible and remained there for some time for all present to witness.

Perhaps one of Estelle Roberts most remarkable achievements came when she was asked by a friend to assist in tracing Mona Tinsley, a ten-year-old girl who had gone missing in Newark-on-Trent, Nottinghamshire in 1937. Having obtained an item of the child's clothing from the Newark-on-Trent Police, Estelle recalled how 'As [she] took it from its wrapping, [she] knew at once that Mona was dead'. She spoke with Mona through Red Cloud, and the girl told how she had been taken to a small house and strangled, whilst giving a detailed description of the area. When the Newark-on-Trent Police were contacted, they told Estelle that this information matched the area where the girl had disappeared. Estelle was subsequently driven around the area and, eventually, she recognised the house that Mona had told her about. Entering the building, Estelle felt the child's presence and told the police that they should search the nearby river. Here, they duly found the girl's body, and the owner of the house was subsequently charged with, and later convicted of, murder.

Estelle's mediumship brought her into contact with several eminent people, both alive and dead. Perhaps the most famous of the latter was the spirit of Sir Arthur Conan Doyle (1858–1930). A friend of Conan Doyle's who was was present at the seance asked where the two of them had last met, to which the great author replied 'by accident in a doorway in Victoria Street'. The friend verified that this was true.

3. The Spiritualist Prophet of Cambridge House, 145 Church Road

Cambridge House was the home of William Thomas Stead (1849–1912), one of the original investigative journalists and among the most vocal supporters of Spiritualism. Throughout 1890 he spent many hours in the garden of Cambridge House discussing the existence of God, religion and the supernatural with a young American journalist, Julia Ames. Shortly after her return to America that year, Ames died of pneumonia, although Stead did not learn of her death for almost a year – from a mutual friend.

By 1892, Stead had discovered that he possessed an ability for automatic writing, whereby a medium writes out messages under the control of a spirit. Julia Ames now became his principal spririt control, and, through her intercession, he was able to conduct a series of interviews with the illustrious dead. With Empress Catherine the Great (1729–1796) he discussed the Russian situation at great length, and he was even able to gain the opinions of the late Prime Minister William Gladstone (1809–1898) regarding the 1909 budget! These conversations were published in his magazine *Borderland*, which appeared quarterly from 1893 to 1897. In *Borderland* he also featured the automatic writings of his spirit guide under the collective heading 'Letters From Julia'. His interviews with the dead were a great sensation of their day, and led him to found 'Julia's Bureau', which helped the bereaved make contact with their dead relatives.

Throughout his life, Stead demonstrated an uncanny ability to predict personal and public events, many concerning great disasters at sea. In a story published in 1893 entitled *From the Old World to the New*, he told of a large ocean liner sinking in the North Atlantic after hitting an iceberg, and in an earlier journalistic piece he predicted a terrible disaster if ocean liners were to cross the ocean with insufficient lifeboats. In 1912, Stead was invited to speak about world peace at Carnegie Hall, New York, on April 21. Before he set sail for America, he predicted that something good would come about as a result of his trip, although not in his lifetime.

Stead's prophesies and premonitions were to have a tragic fulfilment, for he was a passenger aboard the *Titanic* when it struck an iceberg and sank in the early hours of 15 April, 1912. Three weeks after the tragedy he appeared to his daughter and secretary with a radiant face and called to them: 'All I told you is true.'

4. Wimbledon Common

In parts Wimbledon Common is lonely and desolate, and one would be little surprised to meet a spectre meandering its way through the thickets and undergrowth.

The actor Edward Silward, whom we are told was famed in the first half of the twentieth century for his 'extremely clever impersonation of a gorilla', was crossing the Common alone one night when a man in convict's clothes suddenly ran across the ground immediately in front of him and then inexplicably disappeared. When discussing the matter with friends Silward was told that many others had seen a similar apparition on the more remote parts of the Common.

In the 18th century the Common was a notorious haunt of footpads and highwaymen, who were only too willing to relieve lone wayfarers of their possessions and even their lives. One of the most infamous was Jerry Abershaw, who was finally brought to justice in 1795. After his execution his body swung from the gibbet that stood on Wimbledon Hill. Even today, when a full moon casts its uncanny glow across the grass and the skeletal trees stand erect and still, Abershaw's ghost appears astride a phantom mount and gallops at great speed across the Common, the dull thud of the beast's hooves clearly audible as the two ride into the night – and into eternity.

Hampton Court

Location   15 miles (24 kilometres) south-west of Charing Cross.
Transport   Trains from Waterloo Main Line Station to Hampton Court
                      Station. Riverboats from Westminster Pier.
Refreshments   Various pubs and restaurants at the entrance. There is also a
                      restaurant in the palace grounds.

The Tudor palace of Hampton Court sits on a picturesque reach of the Thames surrounded by beautiful gardens. I have described its ghosts in chronological order, beginning with its first owner, Cardinal Thomas Wolsey (*c.*1474–1530) and moving through the troubled marriages of Henry VIII, which account for the majority of the hauntings. In this way you can slot each haunting into your tour of Hampton Court Palace without detracting from your enjoyment of its splendour and history.

In 1514 Cardinal Wolsey began the construction of a magnificent palace on the banks of the Thames. He lived in the completed building in regal splendour and entertained on such a grand scale that his hospitality became the talk of Europe. And then came his fall from grace, as he failed to gain an annulment of Henry VIII's marriage to Catherine of Aragon. In a last desperate bid to buy his way back into royal favour the crestfallen cardinal presented his riverside palace to the monarch. Henry gratefully accepted the gift and, once ensconced at Hampton Court, summoned Wolsey to answer charges of treason. Frail in both mind and body, the dejected cleric set off from his see at York but died en route, at Leicester, wishing that he had 'served God as diligently as I have served my King'.

The Return of the Cardinal

As you wander amid the opulent splendour of Hampton Court, or catch your first sight of its Great Hall, towering majestically over the courts and surrounded by a forest of twisted chimneys, you can imagine the bitterness with which Wolsey parted with his jewel on the Thames. There is only one recorded sighting of his ghost, and this was in a somewhat unusual setting. In 1966 an aggrieved member of the public wrote an indignant letter to say that his enjoyment of a Son et Lumière had been marred by the actor playing the part of Cardinal Wolsey. The producer, Christopher Ede, wrote in reply that there had been no actors in the performance and presumed that the man had actually seen Wolsey's ghost.

Henry VIII Moves In

Good King Hal wasted no time in introducing his second wife, Anne Boleyn, to the splendours of Wolsey's palace. She in turn appears to have left a psychic mark upon the building. Servants have seen her shimmering wraith, dressed in blue, drifting forlornly through the passages and chambers.

The King was courting Anne's replacement while she was still alive. Jane Seymour appears to have brought the King genuine contentment, but she was Queen for only a year. On 12 October, 1537, she gave birth to his longed-for son and heir, but died shortly afterwards (from natural causes). On the anniversary of the birth of her son, her ghost is said to drift silently from her old apartments and wander around Clock Court, its head bent in sadness. She has also been seen near the Silver Stick Staircase, dressed in a flowing white gown and holding an unflickering candle. With an eerie glowing face, the spectre glides down stairways, drifts along corridors, passes through closed doors and has shocked some witnesses into resigning from the palace staff.

The Screaming Spectral Queen

The King's next spouse was Anne of Cleves, but it is his fifth wife, Catherine Howard, who provides the next and most dramatic haunting. Though young when she married the King she was certainly sexually experienced; her past lovers were her music master, Henry Mannock, and a youthful nobleman named Dereham. The new Queen found her husband physically repulsive and sought solace in the arms of a young man at court, Thomas Culpeper. Servant's tittle-tattle brought the girl's previous indiscretions to light and eventually her adultery was exposed. The King was incandescent with rage. Culpeper was taken to the Tower of London and in due course executed (as was Mannock), and Catherine was imprisoned in her chambers at Hampton Court.

As she brooded upon her inevitable fate, the poor, terrified girl hatched a plan that might save her neck. If she could just talk to her husband and plead for mercy, he might spare her life. On 4 November, 1541, knowing that the King would be at prayer, she broke free from her guards and raced through the Haunted Gallery to pound upon the locked doors of the chapel, screaming to her husband to allow her an audience. Henry sat cold and unmoved, ignoring her desperate entreaties. Her guards caught her and dragged the hysterical Queen back to her chambers. On 13 February, 1542, at just twenty years of age, Catherine Howard went bravely to the block: 'I die a Queen, but I had rather died the simple wife of Tom Culpeper. May God have mercy on my soul. Pray for me.' She was smiling when the axe fell.

It is, however, that last desperate rush for clemency that her spiritual shade chooses to repeat, and her sobbing screams have often echoed through the Haunted Gallery. Still more dramatic have been the sightings of her spectral form. Dressed in white, with her long hair hanging loose, she drifts swiftly to the chapel door and abruptly vanishes. Some say that a peculiar, icy coldness can be sensed in the doorway itself, and others feel an intense and desperate sadness that hangs heavily in the air.

A New King and a New Ghost

Following the death of Jane Seymour, a spinster lady by the name of Mistress Sybil Penn was appointed foster-mother to her baby, Prince Edward. Her duties includ-

HAMPTON COURT

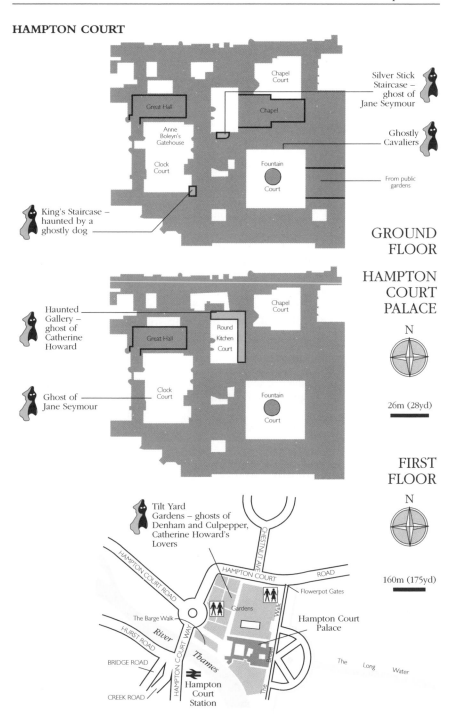

Chapel Court

Silver Stick Staircase – ghost of Jane Seymour

Great Hall

Chapel

Anne Boleyn's Gatehouse

Ghostly Cavaliers

Clock Court

Fountain Court

From public gardens

King's Staircase – haunted by a ghostly dog

GROUND FLOOR

HAMPTON COURT PALACE

Haunted Gallery – ghost of Catherine Howard

Chapel Court

Round Kitchen Court

Great Hall

Clock Court

Fountain Court

Ghost of Jane Seymour

N

26m (28yd)

FIRST FLOOR

N

Tilt Yard Gardens – ghosts of Denham and Culpepper, Catherine Howard's Lovers

160m (175yd)

HAMPTON COURT ROAD

CHESTNUT AVE

HAMPTON COURT ROAD

Flowerpot Gates

The Barge Walk

Gardens

Hampton Court Palace

River

HURST ROAD

Thames

BRIDGE ROAD

HAMPTON COURT WAY

CREEK ROAD

Hampton Court Station

The Long Water

93

ed providing fine clothes for her young charge to wear, and many were the nights when she sat by the light of a flickering candle weaving away at her spinning wheel. When Edward died she retained her chambers at the palace, and she was granted a pension by Elizabeth I. In 1562, both she and the Queen fell ill with smallpox. The Queen recovered but the old nurse died, being buried in the Church of St Mary's Hampton.

In 1829 the church was struck by lightning, and during its subsequent demolition her tomb was desecrated and her remains scattered. This indignity proved too much for Mistress Penn, and ever since her spirit has made its dissatisfaction known in a variety of ways. At the time of the desecration a family named Ponsonby was resident in her old rooms. They complained that their sleep was often disturbed by the whirr of what sounded like a spinning wheel coming from behind the walls of their accommodation. An investigation uncovered a sealed room in which was found a much-used spinning wheel.

The opening of the room appears to have released the spirit, and Mistress Penn has become the most often seen and best attested of all the palace ghosts. She wears a long, grey dress, a hood and a close-fitting cap. She was seen by Princess Frederica of Hanover, who reported that the gaunt figure stood before her with its hands held out as though longing to hold a baby. There have also been reports of shuffling footsteps, of bangs and crashes, of a low humming voice and of her old rooms becoming suddenly bathed in 'a ghastly lurid light'.

Sir Christopher Wren

During the reign of William and Mary that most prolific of architects, Sir Christopher Wren, was employed throughout the last five years of his life supervising rebuilding work at the old Tudor palace. Although he did not die here, it is in the Old Courthouse that his ghostly footsteps are heard on 26 February, the anniversary of his death.

Buried Remains and Ghostly Cavaliers

In the 19th century, Lady Hildyard lived in apartments overlooking Fountain Court. This formidable woman was forever complaining about strange rapping noises in the vicinity of her living quarters. She was even more vociferous in her complaints about two ghostly cavaliers who had the audacity to wander up and down Fountain Court in broad daylight. In 1871 workmen digging in the court came upon two skeletons. Lady Hildyard's investigations convinced her they were those of Lord Francis Villiers and a colleague. She believed they had been killed in a skirmish during the Civil War and hastily buried at the nearest convenient location, which was Fountain Court. The bones were re-buried and since then the spirits appear to have found rest for they have walked no more.

A Policeman Meets a Ghostly Party

In 1907 a policeman on duty at the main gates of the palace noticed a group of men and women coming towards him from the direction of Howe Park. They wore full evening dress, and he presumed that they were returning from an official function.

He turned to open the gates for them, but they suddenly changed their route and began walking towards the Flowerpot Gates, where they just melted into thin air.

Hampton Court has many ghosts and, as you wander its historic chambers, rooms and courtyards, the air bristles with past events. You may meet the ghostly dog that haunts the King's Staircase or the figures of Catherine Howard's lovers, Denham and Culpepper, as they stroll sadly about the tiltyard. There is a distraught grey-haired old woman who runs screaming from the gateway, her long unkempt hair trailing behind and her white dress billowing in the wind as she passes over the bridge. She heads towards the river and suddenly disappears. A pageboy wearing the garments of the reign of Charles II was seen by all the guests at a pre-war garden party. Oblivious to the murmurs of puzzlement he aroused, he strolled happily across the lawn, walked briskly up the steps of the house and promptly disappeared into a solid wall.

History certainly comes alive at Hampton Court, and to walk its fascinating rooms and passages is to walk with kings and queens, lords and ladies, the famous and the forgotten. When the crowds have dispersed and you find yourself alone in a silent corner, attune yourself to the palace's vibrations. Let your mind look back on the happiness and tragedy that its old walls have witnessed. And who knows? There may come a cold draught of air, you may feel the touch of icy fingers on the back of your neck, and some long-dead resident may appear before you, returning once more to their favoured domain.

Windsor and Eton

Transport	Trains from Paddington to Windsor Central Station, changing at Slough
Start	Queen Victoria's Statue, Castle Hill, outside Windsor Castle
Finish	Windsor and Eton Riverside (trains to Waterloo, or a short walk returns you to Windsor Central Station)
Distance	2¾ miles (4.35 kilometres)
Duration	1¾ hours
Best time	At night, when much of the route is deserted
Refreshments	The Two Brewers, by the gate to Windsor Great Park, and the Waterman's Arms, in Brocas Street, Eton.

Dominated by the oldest inhabited castle in Europe, the country towns of Windsor and Eton make an easy excursion from London. Windsor Castle has been the scene of many hauntings but since the majority of these are in areas that are inaccessible to the public, I have covered only those that can be seen from the town itself. Eton is the home of England's top public school, Eton College. Its High Street is lined with delightful buildings from all ages, and there are numerous dark and sinister alleyways that lead to some extremely spooky back streets. Highlights of the walk include a stroll through Windsor Great Park and Windsor Guildhall, a 15th-century building where there is a gruesome reminder of Eton's past as well as magnificent views of the castle itself.

Queen Victoria's Statue

This statue, the starting point of our walk, was placed here in 1887 to commemorate the fiftieth anniversary of Victoria's accession to the throne. It is rumoured that the Queen made frequent attempts to contact the spirit of her dead Consort, Albert, using her loyal servant John Brown as her medium. She dutifully kept detailed records of the seances, and these were found after her death by the Dean of Windsor and destroyed for fear that they might cause a scandal.

With your back to the statue, make your way along Castle Hill and pause by the gates at the top. This is the main visitor's entrance to Windsor Castle, but is locked at night. In April 1906 a sentry who was on duty at the top of the pathway became suspicious of a group of men who appeared from nowhere and walked towards him. Thinking them to be intruders, he challenged them, but they continued to advance, paying him no attention whatsoever. When a third challenge went unanswered, he cocked his rifle and fired at the leading figure. The man paused for a moment, but the group continued their approach. The frantic guardsman raised his bayonet and prepared to charge at which moment the entire group abruptly vanished. He quickly reported his experience to his commanding officer, and a full-scale search of the castle and grounds was instigated, but no intruders were found. As punishment the unfortunate sentry was confined to barracks for three days.

Backtrack along Castle Hill and take the second turning left into Church Street. This delightful cobblestoned street is lined by buildings of differing ages. A little way along on the left is Nell Gwyn's House. Dating from 1640, this was reputedly once the home of Charles II's most famous mistress. Her ghost is sometimes heard, though never seen, moving about the premises.

The Old King's Head

Walk along to the next building. This was built in 1626, and is reputed to be one of the oldest of Windsor's many inns. It was here in 1648 that leading Parliamentarian officers met to resolve that King Charles I 'should be prosecuted for his life as a criminal person'. A reproduction of the signed death warrant can be seen on the wall of the building.

Continue, turning right into Church Lane, where a little way along on the left is Codey's. On its picturesque frontage, is the claim that the building was erected in 1423. This cosy, atmospheric restaurant has in recent years suffered little from the ghost that haunted the premises when it was home to the Engine House Restaurant, in the early 1980s. It was then that a member of staff told the *Windsor and Eton Express* about a ghostly figure that had appeared before her wearing 'a stiff white collar, a hat like a Quaker… he had long flowing hair and a beard'. Without uttering a word the ghost just appeared before her and abruptly vanished. The manageress told the newspaper that staff often heard somebody moving about upstairs. Most disturbing, however, was the large male footprint that would often appear in the bath, although no men were either living in or working on the premises at that time.

Black Horse Yard

Backtrack along Church Lane and go right into St Alban's Street. A little way along on the right you pass the dark and gloomy churchyard of the Parish Church of St John. Just past this, on the left, is the forecourt of The Royal Mews, where several royal coaches are kept. Keep straight ahead into Park Street, one of Windsor's most architecturally distinguished thoroughfares, lined with mostly 18th-century houses and once the beginning of the main Windsor to London road.

Some way along, on the right, you come to the massive wooden gates of Black Horse Yard, named for an old inn that once stood on this site. Local legend tells of a ghostly coach that, at night, comes galloping from this dismal passageway. Drawn by two huge black horses, it turns abruptly right and speeds off towards the gates of Windsor Park, where it melts slowly into the darkness. It is said to contain the ghost of one of the royal physicians who raced to treat the dying King Charles II. Since then, the apparition is supposed to appear just before the death of a monarch, although its last manifestation was in 1910, just before the last illness of Edward VII.

Continue along Park Street, passing on the left the Two Brewers pub, a particularly pleasant and atmospheric hostelry. Go through the Cambridge Gate into

WINDSOR AND ETON

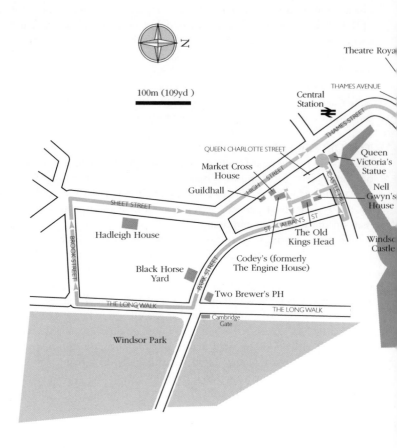

Windsor Park, and towards the locked gate on the left. Here you are afforded a truly majestic view of Windsor Castle's south façade. At night the section of the Long Walk that leads to it is eerily dark and superbly sinister.

The Ghostly Suicide
In 1927 a young sentry on guard duty shot himself through the head in the early hours of the morning. Some weeks later, a colleague of his named Sergeant Leake was given the Long Walk as his sentry duty. Towards the end of what had proved an uneventful shift, Leake was glad to hear the approaching footsteps of what he presumed to be his relief. Instead he found himself looking at the sad face of the young suicide. As he stood staring in bewildered astonishment, the genuine relief guardsman marched into view and the apparition immediately vanished. Back at barracks, Leake told his experience to the sentry whom he had relieved and was informed that he, too, had seen the ghost of the young suicide.

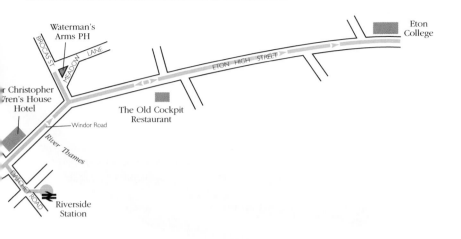

With your back to the gates, stroll along the Long Walk. Ahead of you stretch the 4,800 acres (1,800 hectares) of Windsor Park. Massive trees line your way. Above your head, airplanes begin their descent into Heathrow Airport. This was once the fringe of Windsor Forest, a favoured hunting ground for successive monarchs, and it is to that period of history that Windsor's most famous haunting belongs.

Herne the Hunter

The legend is that Herne was a huntsman in the reign of Richard II who one day saved the King from a savage mauling by a stag, at the near cost of his own life. As Herne lay fatally injured, an old man walked out of the forest and claimed that he could save the huntsman's life. Richard promised that, should Herne live, as a reward for his fearless sacrifice, he would be made head huntsman. The royal party watched as the old man bound a pair of stag's antlers to Herne's head and carried him into the depths of the forest.

But Herne's fellow huntsmen were not so impressed. They sought out the stranger and threatened to kill him should Herne live. He told them that there was nothing now that he could do. He said that Herne would recover and be made head huntsman, but promised that he would not hold the position for long. Satisfied, the huntsmen turned to leave. But the old man stepped in front of them. He prophesied that, since they had wished ill on Herne, they were each and every one of them cursed to an early grave.

Herne did recover and was made head huntsman, but he proved so bad at finding sport for his monarch that he was soon dismissed from his post, and in his shame and despair, hanged himself from a great oak in the forest. One by one, his fellow huntsmen died under mysterious circumstances.

But, on certain stormy nights, Herne comes riding from the trees at the head of a ghostly band of huntsmen and following a pack of baying hounds. This wild hunt is said to appear whenever the nation is threatened, although the last recorded appearance was on the night before Edward VIII abdicated in December 1936.

Continue ahead. The exit gate can be easily missed, so watch out carefully. Some way along on the right, across the grass, is a narrow thoroughfare lined with bright orange lights. Head for the lights and exit through the small gate. Before you do so, however, pause and look around. On more than one occasion those who have found themselves walking this way late at night have suddenly become aware of a man wearing a black cape and tall hat who stands watching them. He stares unblinkingly, fixing them with a steely, sinister gaze before turning and fading slowly into the darkness.

Leave the park by the small gate and make your way along eerie Brook Street then turn right onto Sheet Street, and keep walking along the right-hand side.

Hadleigh House

Dating from the late 18th century, this is one of Windsor's finest Georgian buildings. Footsteps are often heard pacing up and down the staircase, loud, violent knocking noises sound from behind the walls all over the house, and one room is said to have a very unfriendly atmosphere.

A former owner came down one morning to find that she couldn't get into the living-room. A carpenter was called; he managed to gain access and found that, during the night, someone had locked the living-room door from the inside.

Continue along Sheet Street, keeping to the left side. Follow it as it swings left onto High Street and keep walking until you reach , on the right, the Guildhall, built by Sir Christopher Wren in 1687. His initial plans included only a set of outer pillars, which he was convinced would be sufficient to support the upper floors. The town council, however, were not convinced, and insisted he include the central pillars. Wren concurred but, as you can see, left a small gap between the columns and the roof so that they would never bear any load!

Market Cross House

On the other side of the Guildhall is this delightful old building, now a pleasant tea room, which leans at what appears to be an extremely precarious angle. It is free-standing (Windsor's only freestanding wooden structure), and the lack of neighbouring buildings to act as support has resulted in this eye-catching slant.

Inside, near to the fireplace, there is a cold spot that customers often notice. In December 1997 a medium told the owners that she could see a little old lady with grey hair stooping over the fireplace at the exact spot where the coldness occurs. Immediately after Market Cross House is Queen Charlotte Street, which, at 51 feet 10 inches (15.8m) long. is reputed to be the shortest street in Britain.

The Theatre Royal

Continue along the High Street and descend past the walls of Windsor Castle. Some distance along on the left you pass the Theatre Royal. The original 19th-century building was destroyed by fire in 1908, and a young girl known only as Charlotte burnt to death in the conflagration. Charlotte has frequently been seen inside the current theatre, which was built to replace the one that burnt down.

Sir Christopher Wren's House Hotel

As the High Street sweeps to the left, away from the castle, it becomes Thames Street. Cross over Datchet Road and continue along Thames Street, where on the left is the Sir Christopher Wren's House Hotel. Although there is no evidence that the great architect designed or ever lived in the building, it certainly is appropriately old. It was owned for much of the 18th century by a local family called Cheshire, whose tenure here was marked by a run of extreme bad luck. Members of the household would fall seriously ill of ailments indigenous to foreign lands that they had never actually visited. A daughter of the house had an illegitimate child who died in infancy, causing her to suffer a nervous breakdown. Her father nearly died from a serious bout of food poisoning that town gossip maintained was caused by a dose of poison administered by his mad daughter. His fortunes took a turn for the worse and he was forced to sell the building.

The moment the family moved out its bad luck ended. But anyone who came to live here suffered similar unlucky episodes, and the house soon gained the reputation of being cursed. As a result it remained empty for much of the 19th century and on into the 20th century, when it was bought by two elderly sisters who turned it into a hotel. Although they suffered no ill effects, one female guest woke up in the early hours of one morning to see a tall figure standing in the darkened room by a chest of drawers. She watched as the figure crossed the room towards the bathroom and abruptly vanished. She maintained that there was nothing in the least bit frightening about the figure. Today the hotel sits neatly set back from Thames Street and curses and hauntings seem to be a thing of the dim and distant past.

Cross over the bridge and turn left into Brocas Street to arrive at the Waterman's Arms. Windsor suffered terribly from the Great Plague of 1665 and the cellar of the Waterman's Arms was commandeered as a local mortuary. The pub suffers from frequent knocking noises from behind the walls and a small boy with long hair has appeared in one of the bedrooms to sit on the end of the bed.

The Old Cockpit Restaurant

Backtrack along Brocas Street and turn left along Eton High Street. Some way along on the right is the Old Cockpit Restaurant. This picturesque 15th-century construction nestles among many other delightful old buildings and was once the setting for the barbaric sport of cock fighting. The original cockpit still exists behind the building, and is one of the few remaining in England. The building is haunted by a little old lady who flits between the tables of the restaurant, as though looking for some lost article. Her manner is unobtrusive, even apologetic, and successive owners have left her to her own devices.

Continue to the end of the High Street, where you can view Eton College. Alternatively, backtrack over the river along Thames Street, then turn left along Datchet Road to arrive at Riverside Station and the end of the walk.

Westminster to Piccadilly

Start	Westminster Underground Station (Circle and District lines)
Finish	Leicester Square Underground Station (Bakerloo, Northern and Piccadilly lines)
Distance	2 miles (3.2 kilometres)
Duration	1¾ hours
Best Time	Can be done at any time, although my preferred time is on Sunday morning when the West End is least crowded.
Refreshments	Gordon's Wine Bar (passed on the walk but only open weekdays) and numerous sandwich bars and cafés in St Martin's Lane.

This eventful walk cuts a swathe through the heart of government and explores the streets around Whitehall before descending into the gloomy depths of the claustrophobic Adelphi arches. It emerges onto the bustling Strand, where a ghost once plagued the Queen's bank, then descends into a subterranean shopping arcade for a magical encounter. The final section leads you on a stroll through theatreland, taking in ghosts that have appeared in several top London theatres. It passes the Banqueting House, all that now remains of Whitehall Palace, and catches glimpses of the Clock Tower of the Palace of Westminster, whose clock better known the world over as Big Ben. Although parts of the route are very crowded, other sections go through quiet and secluded backwaters, where you will be lucky to meet another living soul.

Old Scotland Yard and the Banqueting House

Leave Westminster Underground Station and turn left onto Bridge Street. Cross Victoria Embankment at the traffic lights and go down the broad flight of stairs on the other side of Queen Boadicea's statue. You are overlooking a section of the Thames where a phantom boat, crewed by three men whose faces are hazy and unclear, drifts lazily through the mist and miasma of early autumn mornings. Slowly it glides towards Westminster Bridge and sails beneath it, never to emerge on the other side.

If you stand here on 31 December, as the old year passes into the new, you may glimpse a shadowy figure that springs onto the parapet of the bridge and leaps headlong into the murky waters of the river. Local tradition holds that on that date and at that hour in 1888 Jack the Ripper killed himself by leaping from Westminster Bridge.

Backtrack across Victoria Embankment, turn right off the crossing and continue until you reach the massive and distinctive gates of Scotland Yard, on the left. Designed by Norman Shaw and described by A.P. Herbert as a 'very constabulary kind of castle', the building, which dates from the 1880s, is faced with granite that was quarried by the convicts on Dartmoor.

Formerly the headquarters of the Metropolitan Police, the building housed the Black Museum. Attendants working amidst this gruesome, fascinating collection of crime memorabilia would frequently see the ghost of a hooded woman drifting aimlessly about the museum. One attendant watched mesmerised as the manifestation drifted towards him and vanished when he challenged her, only to reappear on the far side of the room. He then realised, in horror, that she was headless.

Continue and turn left into Horseguard's Avenue, at the end on the left is the Banqueting House, built in 1622, and all that remains of old Whitehall Palace. Among the many ceremonies that were performed in the hall (the spectacular ceiling of which was painted by Rubens) was that of 'Touching for the King's Evil'. The King's Evil was the disease known as scrofula. As early as the reign of Edward the Confessor, it was believed 'the disease' could be cured by the touch of the King, who possessed the divine, hereditary right to serve his people in this way. There are records of dramatic cures being effected. A young gentlewoman, Elizabeth Stephens, miraculously recovered the sight in her left eye when touched by Charles I in 1640. His son Charles II is estimated to have touched 92,107 people during his reign, although in the year before his death the crowd that came to be cured was so great that several were crushed to death.

Above the main entrance, a bust of Charles I commemorates that bitterly cold day in January 1649 when Charles Stuart stepped onto the scaffold, made a brief speech declaring himself the 'Martyr of the People', and was beheaded.

Cross to the centre of Horseguard's Avenue and stand by the statue of Spencer Compton, eighth Duke of Devonshire. With your back to the statue, look across Whitehall to Horseguards, the finest remaining example of Palladian architecture in central London. In 1901, the Duke of Portland was organising Edward VII's coronation procession when one night he dreamt that, as the coronation coach passed under the arch at Horseguards, the crown at the top became stuck fast against the roof, bringing the entire procession to an embarrassing halt. So vivid was the dream that he decided to measure both the coach and the arch. He discovered that, since Queen Victoria's coronation, the ground beneath the arch had been raised. Had it not been for his precognitive dream the procession would have been halted here.

The Wraith that Haunts the Admiralty Building

Continue along Whitehall, cross over Whitehall Place, and outside number 55 (the Ministry of Agriculture, Fisheries and Food) look across the road at the dark brick Admiralty building. This was built by Thomas Ripley in the 1720s and later enlarged to become Admiralty House, home of the First Lord of the Admiralty. In the latter half of the 18th century the office was held by the Earl of Sandwich, who lived here with his mistress, Martha Ray. She had also become involved with a penniless soldier, later to be an equally penniless clergyman, James Hackman. When Hackman failed to persuade Martha to leave Sandwich, his love turned to insane jealousy. One night, as she left the performance at a Covent Garden theatre, Hackman came rushing from the shadows, drew his pistol and shot her dead. Her ghost has haunted the Admiralty building ever since, and was reputedly seen earlier this century by both Winston Churchill and Harold Macmillan.

In June 1969, several newspapers reported that the politician Denis Healey, then Secretary of State for Defence, and his family were being visited by her restless spirit. Healey was said to have seen her ghost on several occasions in the living quarters at the Admiralty. He also told reporters that, far from being frightened by her, his children were very fond of 'the lady' and had come to accept her as another member of the family.

Continue along Whitehall and cross over Great Scotland Yard, named for the London palace of the Scottish kings that once stood here. In the summer of 1829 the newly founded Metropolitan Police established its headquarters in buildings that adjoined the street, since when the two names have been inextricably linked.

The National Liberal Club's Poltergeist

From Great Scotland Yard go first right into Scotland Place, left into Whitehall Place and pause on the corner of Whitehall Court, outside the National Liberal Club. Built in the 1880s, this massive, turreted building is a local landmark that frequently catches the attention of passers-by on the nearby Victoria Embankment. During the 1890s the rooms occupied by the secretary of the club were disturbed by strange knocking noises that seemed to emanate from deep within the walls. The family carried out extensive investigations and by a careful process of elimination discovered that the phenomenon only ever occurred when a certain German servant girl was in the vicinity. Although convinced that she was in no way consciously responsible for the sounds, the secretary sacked the unfortunate girl and the mysterious noises ceased immediately.

Gordon's Wine Bar and the Ghost of Pepys and Others

Continue to the end of Whitehall Place, go over the pedestrian crossing at Northumberland Avenue and keep ahead to the right of the Playhouse Theatre, passing through the shopping concourse of Embankment Place. Turn left into Villiers Street and, just after the garden railings, go right through the iron gate to pass down the steps to the wine bar.

This deliciously eccentric establishment, once a favoured haunt of the writer Rudyard Kipling (1865–1936), has been referred to as 'the tavern time forgot'. The accumulated dust of decades and the yellow glow from a forest of beautifully evocative candles greet you as you descend a steep flight of worn stairs into this atmospheric basement. Pipes clad in ill-fitting lagging meander across the blackened ceilings, cobwebs cling to model Spitfires and yellowed copies of old newspapers cling to the walls announcing nostalgic headlines such as 'ALEXANDRA PALACE BURNS' or 'MRS SIMPSON READY TO GO ABROAD'. In places the paint peels from the walls, in others the walls peel from the paint. Beneath the low brick ceiling of the cavernous vaults, staff have frequently had the unnerving impression that something is watching them from the darkness, and customers have complained of an unseen hand that taps them on the shoulder as they sit enjoying a glass of wine.

**WESTMINSTER
TO PICCADILLY**

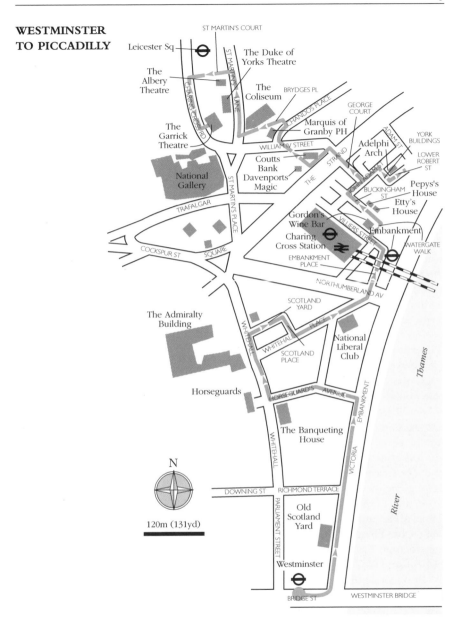

Leave and turn left along Watergate Walk, which until the construction of the Embankment in the mid-1860s would have been lapped by the waters of the Thames. On the right you come to the York Watergate, built for George Villiers, Duke of Buckingham, in the mid-1620s. A gate to the side leads into Embankment Gardens, whose history can be read from the plaque there.

With your back to the Watergate, go up the stone steps and pass through the iron gates into Buckingham Street. The first house on the left, number 14, was the home and studio of the Victorian artist William Etty (1787–1849), who painted sensuous nudes. The 'happy, female ghost' that appears in the hallway from time to time is thought to be one of his models. A little further along, at number 12, the great 17th-century diarist Samuel Pepys (1633–1703) lived 1679–88. His ghost, 'a greyish figure, with a smiling kindly face', often strolls briskly down the stairs or looks down onto passers-by from the first floor windows.

Continue to the top of Buckingham Street and turn right into John Adam Street. Go first right into York Buildings, then first left into Lower Robert Street, which descends into the only surviving Adelphi arch. The area was developed between 1768 and 1774 by Robert, James and William Adam, and the problem of building on land that sloped steeply to the Thames was overcome by building great rows of arches to support the riverside streets. Dickens wrote in *David Copperfield,* 'I was fond of wandering about the Adelphi, because it was a mysterious place with those dark arches' while another account reflected that 'the most abandoned characters… often passed the night [there], nestling upon foul straw'. Among them was a Victorian prostitute known simply as 'Poor Jenny'. She was strangled by one of her clients and left to die on the grim bundle of filthy rags she called home. Today, her pain-racked screams of terror and the rhythmic drumming of her feet still echo through the grimy vaults.

The Haunting of Coutts Bank

Retrace your footsteps back to John Adam Street, cross into George Court, go up the steps, cross over the crossing and go left along the Strand to stop outside the modern glass frontage of the largest of London's private banks, whose most illustrious customer is Her Majesty the Queen. In November 1993 the directors of the bank took the unusual step of calling in the medium Eddie Burks in the hope that he could lay to rest the ghost whose night-time antics were wreaking havoc in the computer rooms. He had even appeared before a receptionist, minus his head. A bank spokesperson told *The Times* how a small number of staff had reported 'strange happenings… like lights going on and off… and an apparition, a shadow was how it was described.'

In the course of a seance Burks made contact with the ghost and learnt that it was Thomas Howard, 4th Duke of Norfolk, whose plot to marry Mary Queen of Scots and depose Elizabeth I had led to his execution in 1572. He told Eddie Burks, 'I was beheaded on a summer's day. I have held much bitterness and… I must let this go. In the name of God I ask your help. I cannot do this alone.'

Burks successfully persuaded the spirit to depart and, on 15 November, 1993, a congregation that included the present Duke and Duchess of Norfolk gathered at a nearby church to offer prayers for the soul of Thomas Howard. As he left the church the present Duke was asked by a reporter if he was glad that his ancestor could now rest in peace. 'Actually,' he replied, 'I don't believe in ghosts.'

Davenports

Continue along the Strand, keeping your eyes open for the ghost of Baroness Burdette Coutts, whose figure, distinguished by her old-fashioned Edwardian dress, has often been seen on this stretch of road. Two doors along, go right down the stairs into the subway shopping area and turn right. Here is Davenports, the oldest family magic business in the world. From the moment the dull thud of a loud bell announces your arrival, you find yourself confronted by a veritable cornucopia of all things magical and mysterious. Ferocious-looking arm choppers, complete with severed arms, glimmer behind glass display cases. There are ESP and Tarot cards for initiation into the secretive world of magicians, mediums and psychics. You can even purchase a copy of the first book ever published on the subject of magic, *The Discoverie of Witchcraft*, written in 1584, at a time when the shop's assistants would probably have been burnt at the stake for the demonstrations of sleight-of-hand that they perform for visitors.

The shop is haunted by what is described by one of the staff, Paul Henri, as a 'male presence'. He has often noticed from the corner of his eye someone walking towards the stock room, 'but when I go to investigate there is never anyone there'. Several other staff members have reported similar experiences, and all agree that working alone in the stockroom at any time of the day can be an unnerving experience.

The Soldier in the Coliseum

Turn left out of the shop and go up the numerous stairs. At the top, go left onto William IV Street (the cream building opposite was the old Charing Cross Hospital and is now Charing Cross Police Station). Take the first right into Chandos Place and, after the Marquis of Granby pub, go immediately left into Brydges Place. This dingy, dark, twisting passage ends when you turn right onto St Martin's Lane and stop outside the Coliseum. Designed by Frank Matcham in 1904, this is London's largest theatre, with a seating capacity of 2,558, and is famed as the first theatre in England to have a revolving stage.

For a short time the building was haunted by a World War I soldier whose last evening on leave was spent at a performance here. His ghost was first seen on the day he was killed in action, 3 October, 1918, and on further occasions for the next ten years. As the house lights dimmed for a performance, he would stroll down the gangway, turn into the second row of the dress circle and vanish, suddenly, into thin air.

The Duke of York's Theatre and a Long-Ago Strangling

Cross over St Martin's Lane and continue along the left side to arrive at the Duke of York's Theatre. The ghost of Violette Melnotte, the eccentric wife of the theatre's first manager, Frank Wyatt, is sometimes seen mingling with the audience on first nights at this pretty theatre, which was built in 1892.

A disturbing series of events here in the late 1940s has become legendary in both theatrical and paranormal circles. Among the costumes worn in the play *The Queen Came By* was an old bolero-style jacket that soon gained the sinister reputation of attempting to strangle any actress who wore it. No matter how much it was let out, those who wore it would complain that it would start to shrink, growing tighter and tighter around them. It was finally agreed to hold a seance at the theatre, and one of the mediums saw the clear image of a man attempting to drown a struggling young woman. Eventually her body collapsed, limp and lifeless, and the man removed her clothing, including her bolero-style jacket, and carried the corpse away wrapped in a blanket. The bodice was ultimately acquired by an American collector of Victoriana. When his wife wore the jacket, she also felt an uncomfortable, strangling sensation. Its current whereabouts are unknown.

The Founder of the Albery Theatre

Continue along St Martin's Lane to the Albery, which was built in 1903 by Sir Charles Wyndham whose ghost is often seen inside the building. Actor Barry Jones was once onstage chatting with an actress during a break from rehearsals when an elegantly attired man with wavy grey hair strolled towards them. They moved aside to allow him to pass and, as he did so, he nodded his thanks. Intrigued by the man's old-fashioned appearance, Jones watched as he crossed the stage and turned out of sight. Following him, Jones asked an attendant at the door who the man was. The attendant was adamant that no one had passed him, and furthermore insisted that there was nobody in the theatre who remotely resembled that description. A little later Jones happened upon a portrait of the theatre's founder and suddenly realised that he had seen the ghost of Sir Charles Wyndham.

The Garrick Theatre

Walk through St Martin's Court, turn left onto Charing Cross Road and walk to the Garrick Theatre, which was designed in 1889 by Walter Emden and C.J. Phipps for W.S. Gilbert (of light opera fame). During 1900–1915 the theatre was managed by Arthur Bourchier, who made his mark on theatreland when, in 1903, he refused to admit the drama critic of *The Times* to a performance. Although Bourchier left the theatre in 1915 his ghost has been seen on numerous occasions backstage after the curtain has fallen; he regularly appears by what is appropriately known as the 'Phantom Staircase'. During a recent refurbishment the ghost appeared in the upper levels of the theatre to several of the workmen.

It is here that your walk can end or continue ahead to Trafalgar Square.

Covent Garden

Start	Covent Garden Underground Station (Piccadilly Line)
Finish	Embankment Underground Station (Bakerloo, Circle, District and Northern lines)
Distance	2 miles (3.2 Kilometres)
Duration	1½ hours
Best times	Except for the Theatre Royal Tour and the courtyard of Somerset House, the walk can be done at night, when many of the alley ways around Covent Garden are gaslit and when the labyrinth of dark streets around the Savoy Hotel is particularly dark and sinister.
Refreshments	The Nell Gwyn Pub and numerous sandwich bars, pubs and restaurants around Covent Garden and the Strand.

Originally the site of the Convent Garden that provided produce for Westminster Abbey, the land here was granted to John Russell, Earl of Bedford, in 1552. Over the centuries that followed his family developed the area, culminating in the building of the magnificent piazza that survives today. This walk will give you the opportunity to explore the piazza, a succession of historic streets and a sloping, sinister alley that houses an eerie old pub. It includes a tour of London's oldest theatre at Drury Lane, and perhaps the chance to see theatreland's most famous ghosts and the lively ghost of Lord Nelson. We finish on the banks of the Thames, looking for the naked figure that is said to lure the unwary to a watery grave. You have been warned.

Covent Garden Station and St Paul's Church

On Christmas Eve, 1955, ticket inspector Jack Hayden was writing up the station log, when the door to his office began to rattle. Thinking it was a late-night reveller, lost in the cavernous depths of the station, Hayden called out, 'There's no way through here,' and continued with his work. But the rattling got louder and the irritated inspector finally got to his feet and opened the door. He found himself face to face with a tall man in a grey suit, who wore tight trousers and a homburg-style hat. The man stared without speaking. Then he turned, walked towards the staircase and melted into thin air.

Over the next few years Jack Hayden encountered the same apparition on no fewer than forty occasions. Nor was he the only member of the station staff to see the ghost. In early 1956 he was in the mess room with station worker Rose Ring when a loud scream interrupted their break. Moments later, ticket collector Victor Locker burst into the room, shaking with fear and muttering hysterically, 'A man was standing there... it pressed down on my head... it vanished...'

COVENT GARDEN

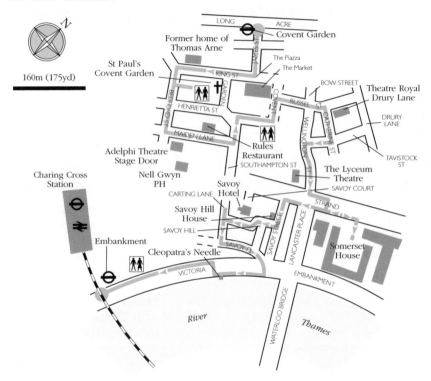

160m (175yd)

Locker's experience and his subsequent refusal to work at the station prompted London Underground to call in Eric Davey, a committed spiritualist. A seance was held, during which Victor Locker suddenly cried out, 'Mr Davey it's on you!' Davey later told the *Sunday Dispatch*: 'I got the name Ter – something.' Somebody suggested 'Terris' and pictures of the Victorian actor William Terris were brought and shown to both Hayden and Locker, who both cried out, 'That's him!' The murder of William Terris is covered later on in this walk (see page 112). His appearances here have been explained by the fact that he was a frequent visitor to a baker's shop that used to stand on the site of Covent Garden Station.

Leave the station, go right into James Street and right again at the Market Piazza, then go straight ahead into King Street. Number 31 was the birthplace of Thomas Arne (1710–1778), composer of *Rule, Britannia* and much else. His father was an undertaker, and Arne used to practice his violin with the music resting on a coffin, much to the horror of violinist Michael Festing, who commented that he would never dare do such a thing in case there was a body in the coffin. Arne smiled and removed the lid to show that there was!

At the end of King Street, turn left into Bedford Street. If the gates a little way along on the left are open, you will come to St Paul's Church. When the church was being commissioned by Francis Russell, 4th Earl of Bedford, he was reluctant to spend a great deal of money and told the designer, Inigo Jones (1573–1652), 'I would not have it much better than a barn.' Jones replied, 'You shall have the handsomest barn in England.' He was true to his word: this airy, spacious church, its walls lined with memorials to famous names connected with the acting profession, today provides a welcome retreat from the general bustle of Covent Garden.

The Murdered Actor of the Adelphi Theatre
Continue along Bedford Street, cross Henrietta Street and go next left into Maiden Lane to arrive, on the right, at the stage door of the Adelphi Theatre.

On 16 December, 1897, William Terris, a genial, generous, popular actor-manager, arrived at the stage door (above which a rather battered royal coat of arms can now be seen) for the evening performance of the play *Secret Service,* in which he was the lead. As he unlocked the door Richard Prince, a bit-part player to whom Terris had shown some kindness but who now had grown to resent him, rushed from the shadows and stabbed him. A crowd soon gathered around the dying man, who lay in the arms of his leading lady, Jessica Milward. As he slipped into unconsciousness, Terris whispered his barely audible last words, 'I will be back.'

In 1928 a tourist walking along Maiden Lane encountered a figure dressed in 'old-fashioned turn of the century clothes'. He was about to make some comment about the man's outdated fashion sense when the figure suddenly vanished into thin air, 'like a bubble bursting'. Later, when shown a picture of Terris, the tourist immediately recognised him as the man he had seen in Maiden Lane. In the same year, an actress resting one afternoon in her dressing room between performances was gripped by the arms, and the chaise longue on which she lay lurched violently from side to side. A mysterious green light appeared above the dressing-room mirror, there were two loud raps that appeared to come from behind the mirror, and then all went quiet. She later discovered that her dressing room was the one that Jessica Milward used to occupy, and that, whenever he passed it, Terris would always knock twice on the door.

The Possessive Ghost of the Nell Gwyn
Continue along Maiden Lane and turn right into Bull Inn Court. This wonderfully sinister alley slopes between the cliff-like walls of the Adelphi Theatre on the right and the Vaudeville Theatre on the left. It isn't difficult to see why it was once a favoured haunt of footpads and cutthroats.

At the end of the alley is the Nell Gwyn, a tiny, dark, atmospheric pub that is one of Covent Garden's best-kept secrets. To the left of the bar, staff and customers often feel a strange coldness hanging in the air, while several gentlemen have felt a hand tap them on the back trouser pocket but turned to find nobody there. A medium once told the landlord that she could see an old man in a cloth cap standing by the stairs, and sensed that he was very pleased with the way the pub was being treated. She said that, should the old man ever be unhappy with the way his building was being treated, he would stop at nothing to drive away those he held responsible. Interestingly, in recent years several landlords who attempted to change the pub's appearance ended up leaving for unspecified reasons.

111

Rules's Haunted Loo

Return to Maiden Lane and turn right. On the opposite side of the road is Rules, reputedly London's oldest restaurant. Founded in 1798 by Thomas Rule, it numbers among its past clientele the writers Charles Dickens, H.G. Wells and Sir Arthur Conan Doyle, as well as Edward VII and his mistress Lillie Langtry, who came so often that a special door was added to enable them to enter unobserved. Still a favourite haunt of writers and actors, it has a wonderful atmosphere. A modest, ghostly prankster haunting the ladies' toilet adds to the ambience. Often a certain cubicle door has been known to slam shut and the toilet heard to flush, despite the fact that there is never anybody in there.

The Theatre Royal, Drury Lane

Continue to the end of Maiden Lane and go left into Southampton Street, passing on the left number 27, formerly the home of the great 18th-century actor David Garrick. Once back at Covent Garden, turn right along the cobblestones and go counterclockwise around the piazza, exiting right onto Russell Street. Cross, and then go over Bow Street and keep ahead to arrive at the Theatre Royal. This is the oldest working theatre in London. The present building dates from 1812, although the original was founded on this site in 1663.

In keeping with its antiquity, the theatre has several ghosts, the most famous being 'The Man in Grey'. This limping apparition, wearing a powdered wig, grey riding cloak and three-cornered hat, always appears at the beginning of a successful West End run. *The King and I, South Pacific* and *Oklahoma* are just three of the musicals he has endorsed, whereas the long-running *Miss Saigon* was blessed with an appearance each time there was a change of cast.

His identity is the subject of much debate. Some say he is the manifestation of Arnold Woodruffe, murdered at the theatre by the actor Charles Macklin two hundred years ago. Another theory is that, when the theatre was being refurbished in the 19th century, a bricked-up room was discovered. Inside was the skeleton of a man with a dagger protruding from his rib cage and fragments of grey cloth hanging on his bones.

Whoever he was, today he is one of theatreland's best-known and best-loved ghosts. His antics, which include pushing actors to positions where they can deliver their lines to the best advantage and deciding to take an afternoon stroll across the stage in front of an entire matinée audience, have become the stuff of theatrical legend.

The Severed Head in the Lyceum Theatre

Leave the Theatre Royal's main entrance, go left along Catherine Street, take the first right and then left into Wellington Street, where a little way along on the right is the newly refurbished Lyceum. A hundred years ago, the rafters of this elegant theatre echoed to the thunderous applause of audiences who had come to enjoy lavish productions of Shakespeare's plays performed by Henry Irving and Ellen Terry.

One couple, however, were treated to a grisly appearance in the 1880s when, during an interval, they looked over the balcony and saw the severed head of a man

Plate 16: The Tudor gate-house of St James's Palace. The palace was the scene of a gruesome 19th-century murder, still re-enacted by the wraith of the victim (see page 68).

Plate 17: 50 Berkeley Square, the most haunted house in London, where a hideous entity lurked in the upper rooms (see page 69).

Plate 18: 19 St James's Place. A ghostly Victorian Lady returned here to escort the soul of her dying sister on its final journey (see page 69).

Plate 19: Holland Park's Holland House where the appearance of three drops of blood always preceded the manifestation of the headless 17th-century Earl of Holland (see page 78).

Plate 20: The former Old Burlington pub in Church Street, Chiswick, home to a good-humoured harmless ghost called Percy (see page 85).

Plate 21: Chiswick House, Lord Burlington's Palladian villa built in 1725, where the mysterious smell of ghostly fried bacon often hangs in the air (see page 84).

Plate 22: The Tudor palace of Hampton Court is inhabited by an array of stately ghosts from the period, including its founder Cardinal Wolsey and several of the six wives of Henry VIII who took over the palace after Wolsey's fall from grace (see page 91).

Plate 23: Henry VIII's fifth wife, Catherine Howard, executed on her husband's orders, is Hampton Court's most dramatic ghost (see page 92). This postcard portrays a simulated ghostly figure that purported to be her.

Plate 24: *In front of Windsor Castle's south façade lies the Long Walk where the ghost of a young soldier has been seen by guardsmen (see page 98).*

Plate 25: *Windsor's statue of Queen Victoria who allegedly held her seances at the Castle (see page 96).*

Plate 26: *The ghost of Nell Gwyn (spelt 'Gwynn' on the façade) is sometimes heard in her former Windsor home (see page 97).*

leering at them from a lady's lap in the stalls below. Their curiosity aroused, to say the least, they attempted to approach the woman after the performance but lost her in the crowd. Some years later, the husband happened to visit a house in Yorkshire where, to his surprise, he saw a portrait of a man whose face was identical to the one he had seen at the Lyceum. Asking who the man was, he was told that it was an ancestor of the owner of the house who had been beheaded for treason, and that his family had owned the land upon which the Lyceum Theatre stood.

Somerset House and Lord Nelson's Ghost

Go left onto the Strand and cross the two pedestrian crossings, then bear left and turn right through the main gate of Somerset House. Originally the palace of Protector Somerset, the current building dates from 1775 and was designed by the architect Sir William Chambers (1726–1796). The statue in the quadrangle depicts George III steadying the rudder as he steers *Britannia* through a troubled sea.

Somerset House was originally home to various offices of the Admiralty. Horatio Lord Nelson (1775–1805) was a frequent visitor, and came here to receive orders to engage the forces of Napoleon at Trafalgar. Having achieved victory, he was mortally wounded in the battle. On bright summer mornings his glowing, feeble form with an empty sleeve swinging by his side is seen almost skipping across the uneven stones of the courtyard, and a wispy, transparent, cloud hovers above his head. If anyone approaches him, Nelson vanishes as suddenly as he appeared.

Savoy Hill House

Leave Somerset House, go left along the Strand and cross over Lancaster Place by the pedestrian crossing. Take the first left along Savoy Street, then go right onto Savoy Hill; almost immediately on the left is Savoy Hill House. In 1923 this building became the first home of the BBC – before that it had been a block of flats. In 1918 the actress Billie Carleton collapsed and died in her room here after returning home from a Victory Ball. The office that replaced her flat is said to be much troubled by ghostly activity, and staff have come to accept that a certain door will often open and close of its own accord, as though some unseen presence had just entered the room.

Continue along Savoy Hill and pass the Savoy Chapel, which is owned by Her Majesty the Queen. Pass into Savoy Way and turn right up the steps of Savoy Buildings. Above your head a multitude of massive pipes twist their way around the outer walls of the Savoy Hotel. This, dark, sinister passage is a million miles away from the opulence and extravagance to be found on the other side of those walls.

The Savoy Hotel's Wooden Cat

Standing on the site of John of Gaunt's Savoy Palace, the Savoy Hotel opened in 1889, and its name soon became synonymous with wealth and privilege. The actor Sir Henry Irving (1838–1905) lived here; Edwardian millionaires thought nothing of flooding its courtyard with champagne; Caruso (1873–1921) sang here and Mae West (1893–1980) held conversations with her mother's ghost in one of the bedrooms.

In 1898 diamond king Joel Woolf held a dinner party at the Savoy prior to his return to South Africa. It was noted that there were thirteen people at the table but, as he got up to leave, Woolf contemptuously dismissed a comment that the first to leave would be the first to die. Within two weeks he was shot dead in his office in Johannesburg. Fearful that further parties of thirteen might risk similar tragedy, the management of the Savoy commissioned a wooden cat to be carved from a single piece of London plane. They named him Kaspar. Now, whenever parties of thirteen sit down to dine, a fourteenth place is set at their table and Kaspar is brought to sit there with a napkin tied around his neck and a saucer of milk on the table before him. Winston Churchill is said to have been so fond of the wooden feline that, when a high-spirited group of RAF officers kidnapped him and flew him to Singapore during World War II, he ordered its immediate return.

Suicide Tales Concerning Cleopatra's Needle
Go back down the steps and cross over Savoy Way. At the bottom of Savoy Hill turn left onto Savoy Place. Cross over Victoria Embankment via the pedestrian crossing and turn right. After a little while you arrive at Cleopatra's Needle, one of two obelisks set up in 1450BC by Pharaoh Thothmes III at the entrance to the temple of the Sun at Heliopolis in ancient Egypt. It was later moved to Alexandria in 14BC by the Roman Emperor Augustus. The monument's full history is detailed on a plaque attached to the obelisk. Since 1878 it has stood proudly on the banks of the River Thames, flanked by two bronze Victorian sphinxes.

It seems to attract those of a despondent nature, since more suicides take place on this reach of the Thames than on any other. Those passing the towering column have sometimes heard a low moaning emanating from the dark granite, while others have seen a shadowy, naked figure that sprints across the riverside terrace and springs head first over the wall towards the river. But there is never a splash, and those who have the courage to investigate find no trace of a body.

One foggy night in the 1940s a policeman patrolling across Waterloo Bridge was approached by an hysterical young woman who came racing from the swirling fog. She told him that someone was about to kill themselves and begged him to follow her quickly. The constable arrived at Cleopatra's Needle just in time to stop a young woman throwing herself into the murky waters of the racing river. Having pulled the suicide back from the edge, he found himself facing the lady who had just alerted him on Waterloo Bridge. Looking to where she had been standing just two minutes before, he could find no sign of her whatsoever.

The tour ends alongside Cleopatra's Needle. Cross the pedestrian crossing, go left and arrive at Embankment Underground Station.

Gaslit Ghosts, the Temple and Fleet Street

Start	Blackfriars Underground Station (Circle and District lines and British Rail Main Line)
Finish	Temple Underground Station (Circle and District Lines)
Distance	2½ miles (4 Kilometres)
Duration	1½ hours.
Best Times	Evenings and weekends
Refreshments	Ye Olde Cheshire Cheese (closed on Sunday nights). Various fast-food outlets and pubs passed en route.

This walk will take you through the enchanting Middle Temple and Inner Temple before steering you in and out of some wonderfully sinister alleyways along Fleet Street. At night the Temple area is lit exclusively by gaslight, and the deserted courtyards, lined by 18th- and 19th-century buildings, are eerie and magical. Fleet Street is a busy thoroughfare, yet a sequence of menacing alleyways and courtyards that runs off it spirits you back to the days of Dickensian London, and it comes as little surprise to learn that you are wandering through the grisly realm of Sweeney Todd. This route is best saved for a Saturday night, when most of it is totally deserted. The only drawback is that the Temple Church will be closed. However, once you have discovered this wonderful and historic area you will certainly want to return during the day.

The Hanging Judge of the Temple

Leave the station via exit 8 onto New Bridge Street, go first left into Watergate, right onto Kingscote Street and left along Tudor Street. The route takes you between rather uninspiring high-rise office blocks, but at the corner of Dorset Rise a dazzling view of the Wedding Cake spire of St Bride's Church awaits. Continue along Tudor Street, cross Carpenter and Carmelite streets, and go straight ahead through the archway to enter the Temple. Pass into this tranquil oasis and you find yourself walking among buildings and courtyards that time and progress have left untouched. Admittedly, the ethereal glow from countless computer screens detracts slightly from the romance and provides a sharp contrast to the atmospheric dark, brick façades and stately windows that surround you.

You have entered the Inner Temple, one of London's four Inns of Court. Here, barristers (the advocates of the legal profession) have their offices or chambers in buildings that date from the 18th and 19th centuries. At night the area is even more enchanting, lit by the almost magical glimmer of gaslight. Go through the gates, walk diagonally and right, across the huge courtyard. When you arrive at the red pillar box, pause and look around.

In the early hours of winter mornings, when the buildings are empty and the yellow light of the gaslamps casts peculiar shadows across their façades, one former resident, Hanging Judge, Henry Hawkins (1817–1907), returns to wander where he once walked in life. He appears in the hours after midnight, wigged and robed and with a mass of dusty legal papers clutched in his arms, and rushes at a brisk pace past startled onlookers. As he walks his image begins to fade until, after a few tantalising moments, he has dissolved into the night.

The Mystery Skeleton of Middle Temple Hall

Continue along the pavement. To your right is the relatively modern Inner Temple Hall, rebuilt in the 1950s, its predecessor having been razed by the bombs of the Blitz. Pass through the arch and turn right into Middle Temple Lane to arrive at Middle Temple Hall, on the left. Middle Temple is another of the Inns of Court. The dining hall, which was built in 1573, is notable architecturally for its double hammer-beam roof, and was used as the venue for the first-ever production of *Twelfth Night* on 2 February, 1602. During renovation work in the latter half of the 19th century, workmen were intrigued to find an old box hidden in a recess near the roof with a human skeleton inside it. Who put it there, and why, are questions that have never been resolved.

The Temple Church and Ye Olde Cock Tavern

Continue along Middle Temple Lane and go right under the arch. Pass through Pump Court, noting the sundial on the wall, dated 1686, with its salutary inscription: 'Shadows We Are and Like Shadows Depart'. Go through the cloisters to arrive at the Temple Church.

From the 12th to the 14th centuries, the area now occupied by the Middle and Inner Temples was the London citadel of the Knights Templar. This monastic military order, founded in 1118 to protect pilgrims on the road to Jerusalem, would later find glory as the soldiers of Christ on the battlefields of the Crusades. This church, which is all that remains of their tenure here, is said to be one of the most psychically charged buildings in London. Built in 1185, it has a round design based on the Holy Sepulchre in Jerusalem.

Stand by the Norman doorway to experience the atmosphere of the church. Note one curious section on the opposite side above the colourful tomb of Edmund Plowden (1518–1585 – the man who built the Middle Temple Hall). This narrow slit in the wall was the penitentiary cell, where disobedient members of the order were locked in cramped confinement and starved to death. Psychics say that a feeling of intense anger pervades the air around this particular spot.

Leave the church and go clockwise to its rear courtyard. Keeping Goldsmith's Building on your left, stop by the nondescript black door that bars your way. This is the back door of Ye Olde Cock Tavern, and it was here that the ghost of the writer Oliver Goldsmith (1728–1774) once put in a rather startling appearance. (Goldsmith is buried over by the railings to your right.)

GASLIT GHOSTS, THE TEMPLE
AND FLEET STREET

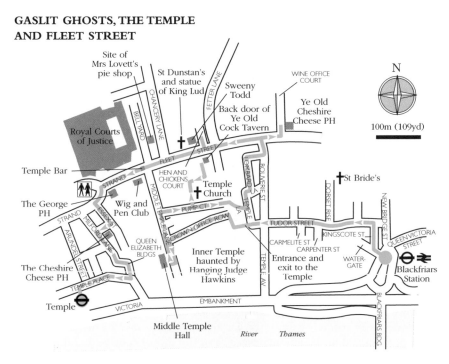

One night in October 1984 an Australian barmaid opened the back door to put out the rubbish and found herself face-to-face with the disembodied head of a man, hovering in mid air and grinning at her. With an almighty scream she raced back into the pub in hysterics. Sarah Kennedy, the landlady, calmed her, and suggested she go upstairs to lie down. The girl had reached the first-floor landing when she started screaming again. As staff rushed to her assistance, they found her pointing at a portrait of Oliver Goldsmith, stammering, 'That's him… that's the face.'

Ye Olde Cheshire Cheese

Return to the front of the church and, with your back to the cloisters, walk through the covered passageway opposite. Bear right, cross the courtyard and leave the Temple through the gates. Turn immediately left into Temple Lane, then left into Lombard Lane. Turn right along Fleet Street, cross at the pedestrian crossing, and turn right then left into the third alleyway, Wine Office Court. In this alley is Ye Olde Cheshire Cheese. Rebuilt in 1667, this rambling, atmospheric old tavern stands above a warren of cellars and basement rooms that predate the upper floors by over a hundred years. From its dark wooden walls, portraits and photographs of those who have worked or supped here over the centuries gaze fondly down. In the back room, in a glass case perched precariously upon a narrow perch, sits a famed former resident, Polly the parrot, which became world-famous in the 1920s for its ability to swear and curse fluently in nine different languages. Its death, in 1926, was reported by newspapers the world over, and headlines concerning its demise are displayed on the walls of the room.

117

Hen and Chickens Court and the 'Demon Barber'

Retrace your footsteps back to Fleet Street and turn right. Cross over Fetter Lane and take the first turning right into Hen and Chickens Court. This narrow, dark, grimy passageway takes its name from an inn that once stood here. It opens into an even grimier, Dickensian courtyard, where a muddle of off-white buildings are apparently held together with rusting slabs of iron. Beneath your feet, iron grilles cover drops in whose shadowy depths untold horrors might lurk.

Horrors indeed are associated with this place, for you are at 186 Fleet Street, the premises of Sweeney Todd, 'The Demon Barber of Fleet Street'. Todd was careful about selecting special clients. They had to be from the countryside, or better still from abroad – people who, in the days when news travelled slowly, would go unmissed for the longest periods of time. They would sit and relax in his barber's chair, and Todd would begin to shave them. Suddenly, he would pull on a lever, the chair would tip backwards, and the hapless customer would be pitched heels over head through a trapdoor into the dark of the cellar below. As they lay, stunned, the Demon Barber would rush at them and dispatch them with one slash of his razor. Their bodies would then be dragged through an underground tunnel to nearby Bell Yard, where his accomplice, Mrs Lovett, kept a pastry shop that sold the tastiest meat pies in London!

Sadly, Sweeney Todd never actually existed outside Victorian melodrama, but the bloodthirsty nature of the story has kept his name alive to this day. Late at night, as you stand in the gloomy darkness of this dismal courtyard, you could be forgiven if you mistook the occasional shadow, passing behind you, for the rush of a sinister figure.

King Lud

Returning to the safety of Fleet Street, turn right and keep ahead, passing the Church of St Dunstan's in the West. Its magnificent clock dates from 1683 and is reputedly the oldest in London. The two giants on either side strike the quarter hours, although they often hammer out the hour when it is some fifteen or twenty minutes past. The porch to the right of the clock is home to three of London's oldest statues, those of King Lud and his two sons. Lud was the legendary King who is supposed to have built Lud Gate, hence the name of nearby Ludgate Hill. He is said to lie buried in a secret vault, deep beneath the site of his gate. The statues are thought to be over six hundred years old.

Cross over Chancery Lane and Bell Yard to arrive at Temple Bar on the right. This mid-road monument marks the end of Fleet Street and the start of the Strand, which is the point where the City of London ends and the City of Westminster begins. It replaces the original Temple Bar, which now decays, forgotten and neglected, in Theobald's Park in Hertfordshire. The heads of executed criminals used to be placed above it as a gruesome reminder to all those who entered the City of the fate that befell those who misbehaved. The heads, picked at by the crows and pigeons, became a sideshow in the 17th century, when an entrepreneur set up a business renting telescopes to enable his fellow citizens to get a closer view.

The Royal Courts of Justice

The pinnacled and turreted buildings to your right are the Royal Courts of Justice, usually known as the Law Courts, opened in 1882 and designed by the architect George Street (1824–1881) who, sadly, worked himself to death before seeing his building completed.

Before the Law Courts were built, a tangle of sordid, tiny, winding passages and overcrowded courtyards stood on the site. So intricate was this maze that small boys could make a reasonable living guiding strangers through it. One young man refused to pay for their guidance and set off alone into the alleyways. He was never seen alive again, but his ghost was often glimpsed trying desperately and unsuccessfully to find its way through the labyrinth, always fading away as daylight crept through his nocturnal haunts.

The Wig and Pen Club Ghost

Cross over the Strand at the pedestrian crossing, and bear left to the Wig and Pen Club. The timbered front of this 17th-century survivor is dwarfed by the massive Edwardian buildings that surround it. A private club for lawyers and journalists, it is haunted by the sound of ghostly footsteps pacing anxiously up and down the ground-floor corridors in the early hours of the morning. They are reputed to represent the nervous meanderings of a solicitor who worked himself to death in his offices during the reign of Queen Victoria.

The George Tavern

Walk along the Strand towards the Church of St Clement Danes and stop on arrival at the black-and-white timbered frontage of the George Tavern. The pub dates from the 1930s but stands on much older foundations, where a ghostly manifestation has frequently been seen. During a refurbishment in the 1970s a gang of painters and decorators arrived to start work. The foreman allotted various tasks to his men, then went down into the cellar and was soon busily whitewashing the old stone walls. Twenty minutes later he came racing upstairs somewhat flustered. 'That feller down there, gu'vnor, he just looked at me, didn't say nothin', just stared,' he panted. The landlord asked him to describe the man. 'All 'istorical like them Roundheads and cavaliers,' came the breathless reply. 'Oh I shouldn't worry about him,' said the landlord, reassuringly. 'That's the ghost. My wife sees him all the time.'

There have been many times when bar staff changing beer barrels in the cellar have turned to see the ghostly cavalier standing in the shadowy recesses. He is accepted by the staff as a harmless fellow-resident, whom the landlord has nicknamed 'George'.

Leave the pub, turn left onto the Strand, then go first left into Essex Street and right into Little Essex Street where, on the corner, you arrive at the Cheshire Cheese. Lacking the history of its namesake off Fleet Street, the pub has a mischievous ghost who enjoys moving the juke box around in the middle of the night.

Turn left along Milford Lane, follow it into Queen Elizabeth Buildings and turn right into Temple Place. Opposite is Temple Underground Station, where this walk comes to an end.

The Blackfriars Walk

Start	Blackfriars Underground Station. (Circle and District lines. British Rail Main Line)
Finish	St Paul's Underground Station (Central Line)
Distance	1 mile (1.6 kilometres)
Duration	1 hour 10 minutes
Best Times	The walk is best done at night or at weekends, when the work ing population have gone home and the streets are left to you and their ghostly populace.
Refreshments	The Blackfriar (closed at weekends), the Cockpit (open 7 days; located opposite St Andrew by the Wardrobe) and several pubs that line Ludgate Hill. The area is not well served with refreshment stops on weekend evenings.

The district of Blackfriars grew up on land formerly occupied by a great monastery of the Dominican Friars. Many of its ancient streets and sloping alleyways still show the original medieval street patterns. Some of London's most atmospheric places are here. Age-old courtyards with dark stone walls have witnessed London life at its best and worst. Dark, sinister and shadowy alleyways make the bustle of the modern city seem a million miles away. This walk goes through that area before arriving at St Paul's Cathedral, then moves on to a tucked-away courtyard with sinister residents. It is a very short walk and will take little over an hour, but you can combine it with 'The City of the Dead' (pages 33–7) to create a walk lasting about 2½ hours.

The Blackfriar Pub

Leave the underground by exit 1 and you will come to what is surely London's most unique pub. This wedge-shaped pub no longer nestles amid the warren of ancient streets that dictated its flat-iron shape, but it stands as a reminder of the area's monas-tic past. Its façade is dominated by a rotund jovial friar, and carved on the walls beneath are a crowd of bibulous monks battling their way to the bar. The interior is very much Arts and Crafts meets Art Nouveau. Bronze bas-reliefs depicting jolly friars enjoying a well-stocked table, or squeezing their krumhorns in choral over-ture, adorn the walls. In the grotto to the side of the bar pagan figures perch in the corners, their legs swinging mischievously over unconcerned drinkers.

The Monastery of the Dominican Friars

Leave the pub and turn left onto Queen Victoria Street, a none too pleasant Victorian thoroughfare that is overshadowed by vast modern office blocks, those on your left standing on the site of the monastery. The monastery was occupied by the friars from 1278 to 1538. They wore black habits and so were known as the Blackfriars, and the name in turn passed to the area.

In 1382 a special council was summoned to meet at the monastery by the Archbishop of Canterbury in order to examine the doctrines of John Wycliffe the religious reformer (*c.* 1329–1384). During the meeting a terrible earthquake shook the city, causing Wycliffe to observe that, although the council had denounced his teachings, God in turn had denounced the council's judgement.

St Andrew by the Wardrobe's Harbinger of Death

Continue along Queen Victoria Street, where there is little of note until you cross St Andrew's Hill and arrive, on the left, at the church. Go up the steps, turn left, then right at the end of the path. Suddenly the 20th century is left far behind and the roar of the traffic is reduced to a distant murmur. The uninspiring offices give way to an oasis of silent shadow where a charming knot of medieval lanes and passageways snake their way between crumbling walls of uncertain age.

Stand beneath the tower of the church and look up. In 1933 three bells were taken from the parish church at Avenbury, in Herefordshire, and hung in this tower. One of them, Gabriel, had been cast in Worcester in the 15th century and had a sinister reputation as a messenger of death. Everyone who lived within the sound of its chime knew that, whenever a vicar of Avenbury died, Gabriel would always ring of its own accord to mourn his passing. Barely a year after its arrival here, local residents were woken early one morning by the knell of a solitary bell, sounding from the tower. The night was still, with not even a faint breeze. A cursory search of the building found no sign of a forced entry. There was nobody inside the church, and the door to the belfry was firmly locked. Many people had heard the ringing, though none could explain how, or why, it could have happened, but the next day word came that, shortly before Gabriel had mysteriously chimed, the vicar at Avenbury had died.

The church interior is rather plain, although there is some interesting stained glass, and the font and pulpit both date from the 17th century. The entrance is by the north door, located at the end of the passage in which you stand.

Leave the church and pass the rectory, which was built in 1766 on the site of the King's Wardrobe. This had been established here in 1359 as the offices and buildings where the Master of the King's Wardrobe looked after state robes and supplied cloth to the royal household. The building's timber construction led to its complete destruction by the Great Fire of London in 1666, after which the Wardrobe was moved to Westminster.

Continue up St Andrew's Hill to the junction with Carter Lane, once one of the City's main thoroughfares. The colourful building opposite is the City of London Youth Hostel, originally the St Paul's Choir School – hence the bright ecclesiastical motifs and Latin inscriptions that adorn the façade.

The Haunt of Wardrobe Place

Turn right into Carter Lane and then right through a covered passageway into Wardrobe Place. This glimpse of bygone London dates from 1720. To stand here on a winter's night, when the lights of the neighbouring buildings have been switched off, is to experience the true thrill of historic and haunted London. Massive plane trees tower over the three-storey houses, and even the faintest of breezes will set their branches creaking and their trunks swaying. The stillness of the yard keeps you constantly on edge, passing darting glances around the gloomy shadows, feeling certain that unseen eyes are watching you from the inky blackness of the house windows.

Not surprisingly, the courtyard has a ghost. People going about their honest, night-time toil in the neighbourhood have reported sighting a lady, dressed all in white, drifting aimlessly from door to door. Who she is and why she should choose to wander this courtyard is unknown. She says nothing, does nothing and pays little heed to anyone or anything, being more than content to let the world pass her by as she goes about her ghostly business. But, should someone be so rude as to stare at her, she takes umbrage and responds by fading into nothingness.

The Old Deanery and the Mystery of the Toilet-Roll Holder

Exit Wardrobe Place, turning right, and take the first left into Dean's Court. A little way along, on the left, is the deanery. This was built in 1670 by Sir Christopher Wren and was formerly the residence of the Dean of St Paul's Cathedral. Local tradition holds this to be a haunted building, a claim vociferously disputed by Martin Sullivan, Dean of St Paul's, until his retirement in 1977. The strange creaks that were often heard by members of his family and staff he put down to the antiquity of the building. The bumps and clanks that were often heard at night he dismissed as 'nothing more than the central heating getting on a bit'. He did, however, confess to being slightly bemused by a toilet-roll holder that would go 'decidedly wonky' whenever anyone else looked at it, but which had always righted itself by the time the Dean was called to repair it. But then he added: 'Since I can't conceive of a haunted toilet-roll holder, I can only put it down to my skill at do-it-yourself.'

Continue along Dean's Court and confront one of London's most awe-inspiring sights, as the west façade of St Paul's Cathedral hoves into view and rises majestically above you. Unfortunately, its appearance also means that the narrow streets and tranquillity of the Blackfriars area are about to give way to the cars and buses that roar up and down Ludgate Hill.

Cross over the pedestrian crossing and make your way to the front of the cathedral. Sir Christopher Wren's masterpiece was completed in 1710, during the reign of Queen Anne, whose statue stands at the front of the cathedral. Tradition holds that the statue is looking to the right towards the gin and beer shops of the area, a reference to the Queen's enjoyment of 'mother's ruin'. Small boys are said to have once danced around the statue chanting: 'Brandy Nan, Brandy Nan, you're left in the lurch, your face to the gin shops, your back to the church.'

The Whistling Ghost of the Kitchener Chapel

Face the cathedral and enter the building through the left door. Almost immediately on the left is the Kitchener Chapel. This can be a somewhat busy throughway, yet the chapel has a tranquillity and stillness about it that the constant barrage

THE BLACKFRIARS WALK

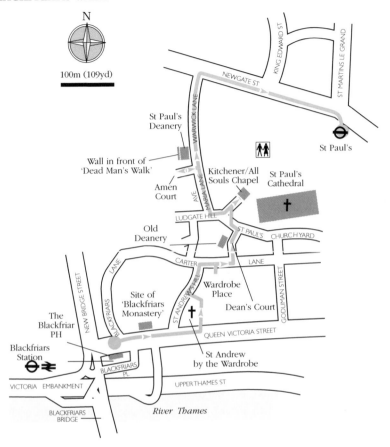

of camera-carrying visitors does little to dispel. Battle colours adorn the walls, and a prostrate, white-marble effigy of General Kitchener (1850–1916) slumbers peacefully upon the stone floor.

In a quiet moment, when there is a lull in the pedestrian traffic, you may just happen to hear the low, barely audible sound of a mournful whistling. Do not ignore it, for it heralds the approach of 'Whistler', the ghost of St Paul's. The first hint that something supernatural is afoot comes when the air about you begins to get cold. Looking round, you may spy a wizened old clergyman with flowing locks of grey hair, dressed in old-fashioned robes. His mournful though tuneless whistling gets louder and louder as he glides across the chapel where, upon arrival at the wall to your right, he melts slowly into the stone. Everyone who has seen him attests that he always follows exactly the same route across the chapel and into the same section of wall.

After the 1914–18 war this chapel, formerly known as the All Souls Chapel, was re-dedicated and renamed the Kitchener Chapel. During the renovation work a secret door was uncovered at the exact spot where the mysterious disappearance always occurs. The door opened onto a narrow, winding, wooden staircase that led to a secret room within the inner fabric of the main body of the cathedral. The only person who appears to have known of its existence, or purpose, was 'Whistler', whoever he may have been in his lifetime.

Leave the cathedral through the same door by which you entered and walk ahead onto Ludgate Hill. Turn first right into Ave Maria Lane. You will pass on your left Amen Corner, leading to Amen Court, where the Chapter of St Paul's live in buildings built by Sir Christopher Wren in the 1680s. Many of the doorways still possess their link extinguishers, from the days before street lights. People going out in the dark would employ a link boy to run before them, lighting their way with a lighted torch, or link. Upon arrival at your door, the boys would extinguish the link and head off in search of another paying client.

Deadman's Walk

Continue along Ave Maria Lane which, a little further along, becomes Warwick Lane. On your left you will arrive at the red brick deanery of St Paul's Cathedral. Gaze through the archway at the large, dark wall that dominates the far side of a peaceful courtyard. Built onto the foundation of the old Roman fortification, this 18th-century structure hides behind it a tiny passageway known as Deadman's Walk. Until 1902, the infamous Newgate Prison loomed large beyond this wall. Prisoners were once led along this passageway to their executions, and buried beneath it afterwards – hence its sinister nickname.

The wall is haunted by the 'Black Dog of Newgate', a shapeless black form that slithers along the top of the wall, slides sloppily down into the courtyard and vanishes. Its appearance is always accompanied by a nauseous smell, and often by dragging footsteps that echo across the garden of the deanery. Its origins go back to the reign of Henry III, when a fearsome famine struck London and the poor felons of Newgate Prison were forced to turn to cannibalism for survival. A scholar was imprisoned on charges of sorcery. Within days of his arrival, his fellow prisoners had killed and eaten him, pronouncing him to be 'good meate'.

However, they soon had reason to regret their actions when a hideous black dog, with eyes of fire and jowls that dripped with blood, appeared in the night and tore hapless prisoners limb from limb. Their anguished, helpless screams echoed through the shadows, striking terror into the very souls of their fellow inmates. Prisoners who heard the beast's ghostly panting and its heavy paws padding along the corridors as it approached their cells, died of fright. Those who survived the first, marrow-chilling nights of its lust for blood and revenge became so terrified that they killed their guards and escaped. But, no matter how far they travelled, the beast hunted them down and killed them one by one. Only when the murder of its master, the sorcerer, had been fully avenged did it return to the prison's foetid dungeons, where it always appeared on the eve of an execution or the night before a prisoner breathed his last, as a hideous harbinger of death.

When the prison was demolished in 1902 it was hoped that the black beast would go too. But it was not to be. People walking in the courtyard at night, or glancing in as they hurry by this silent spot, have reported seeing a seething black mass that shuffles across the wall, slides slowly into the courtyard, and melts into nothingness.

The Reading Baby Farmer

Deadman's Walk has other ghosts. The courtyard ahead of you is haunted by the shade of Jack Shepherd, the 18th-century cat burglar who escaped three times from the prison. His ghost, clad in 18th-century garb, comes leaping from the wall and runs towards startled witnesses, melting into thin air as he draws close.

One of the most detested inmates to have graced the prison with her presence must surely have been old Amelia Dyer, the 'Reading Baby Farmer'. Paid to look after unwanted babies, she would drown her charges in the Thames and other rivers while still drawing money for their upkeep. On the day of her execution, 10 June, 1896, as she was being led to the gallows she passed by a young warder named Mr Scott. Stopping abruptly, she slowly turned her head and fixed him with her evil gaze. Her small, dark eyes looked into his, her face cracked into a toothless smile and, in a low, rasping whisper, she sneered, 'I'll meet you again some day, sir.' Moments later she was dead, dangling at the end of the hangman's rope.

The years passed, Scott progressed in his chosen career, and all thoughts of Mrs Dyer and her prophecy were forgotten. Then one night just before the prison was to close, he found himself alone in the warders' room, his back to the grille that looked out onto Deadman's Walk. Suddenly, a shiver ran down his spine as he got the distinct impression that somebody was watching him. And now he heard again the voice of Mrs Dyer, that unmistakable, sneering rasp: 'Meet you again, meet you again...' Turning, he saw the old lady's face, framed by the grille, grinning at him. A few seconds later she had vanished. He raced to the door and threw it open, only to find that the passage was completely empty.

Had he imagined it? Possibly, yet he never could account for the woman's handkerchief which, at that very moment, fluttered to the flagstones at his feet...

Continue along Warwick Lane and turn right onto Newgate Street where, a little way along, you come to St Paul's Underground Station and the end of the walk.

Southwark

Start	Monument Underground Station (Circle and District Underground lines)
Finish	London Bridge Underground Station (Northern Line)
Distance	3½ miles (5.6 Kilometres)
Duration	1¾ hours
Best Times	The area is at its creepiest at night. Unfortunately this means that the Old Operating Theatre is closed, so late in the afternoon is a good compromise.
Refreshments	The George Inn, Anchor Tavern and Market Porter which are all featured.

Southwark is located immediately over the Thames from the City of London. The name is derived from South Warke or Work; the district was first settled by the Romans 2,000 years ago. As the main approach to London from the south, the area was noted for its inns, and a large proportion of the haunted sites described on the walk are pubs. But Southwark was also famed as the entertainment district for London at a time when the puritanical City of London banned play-acting and other enjoyments in the Square Mile. With the opening of the New Globe Theatre in June 1997 the river banks are now echoing once more to the words of the Bard; although the Globe is not featured on the walk, it is well signposted and can be reached by extending the route a little way from the Anchor Tavern. Parts of the walk takes you through some creepy dark streets and much of it is through extremely historic quarters, so don't rush: stay and savour the area.

The Spectre in St Magnus the Martyr

Leave Monument Underground Station at the Fish Street Hill exit and turn right. Pass the Monument to the Great Fire of London, which started on 2 September, 1666, on Pudding Lane, which is next along on your left. Continue your descent of Fish Street Hill to cross Lower Thames Street, and enter the clearly visible Church of St Magnus the Martyr. Go to the right of the altar, where a plaque on the wall states that the remains of Miles Coverdale (1488–1568) are interred in a vault beneath your feet. Coverdale was the rector of this church from 1563 to 1565, and is best remembered as the man who, when he was Bishop of Exeter, instigated the first English translation of the Bible.

The church attracts few visitors and has a peaceful air about it. But there have been occasions when those near this spot have suddenly felt intense grief. Some have seen the form of a dark-haired priest in a black cassock stooping over the vault where the bishop lies entombed. This has led to the supposition that it is Miles Coverdale himself who haunts the church.

An electrician who spent several days working here complained of a priest who kept watching him and appeared to be there one moment but gone the next. One Sunday evening a verger locked the church and was tidying up when he noticed a priest standing a few feet away from him. He was about to ask how the man had managed to enter a locked building when the figure dropped to its knees and began searching for something on the floor. Stepping forward to offer assistance, the verger was taken completely by surprise when the priest just looked up, grinned at him and vanished into thin air.

Old London Bridge

Having explored the church's spectacular interior, return to Lower Thames Street. The tower through which you leave is sandwiched between modern office blocks but, until 1832, provided the pedestrian access onto Old London Bridge, a few remnants of which lie scattered around the churchyard. Go left along the noisy and busy main road, then left up the stairs that lead to London Bridge. Continue ahead onto the bridge, where a magnificent panorama unfolds before you, with Tower Bridge and *HMS Belfast* dominating the vista. The clearly discernible gap between the offices to your left is where Old London Bridge stood from 1215 to 1832.

There is a tradition that this sweep of the river is haunted by ghostly cries, the result of tragedy caused by Edward I's expulsion of the Jews from England in 1290. One group hired a ship to take them abroad, and it was arranged with the captain that they would set sail from just below London Bridge. Their vessel, however, was caught by the ebb tide and became beached upon the river sands. The captain suggested they leave the ship and await the turn of the tide on a dry sand bank in midriver. But, as the tide began to rise, the captain raced to his ship, leaving his hapless passengers stranded as the waters engulfed them, and one by one they were drowned. The exact spot where the tragedy occurred is uncertain, but there is a strong Jewish tradition that it was beneath London Bridge. One Victorian Anglojewish writer wrote that the spot on the Thames where it happened 'is under the influence of ceaseless rage; and however calm and serene the river is elsewhere, the place is furiously boisterous'.

Retrace your footsteps off the Bridge and, just before the telephone boxes, cross the road via the pedestrian subway. Bear right to cross over London Bridge and on the opposite side go right down the second set of steps into the grounds of Southwark Cathedral.

Southwark Cathedral and the Miserly Ferryman

Long before any bridge spanned the Thames, a ferryman named John Overs had the monopoly of ferrying cargoes and passengers across the river, and in the process he became immensely wealthy. But he was also a tight-fisted miser. His servants were treated very badly, and his only daughter, Mary, was forbidden to marry the man she loved because her father refused to provide a dowry. One day it occurred to John Overs that, if he pretended to be dead for twenty-four hours, his household would mourn, and their fasting would save him the cost of a day's food. He therefore wrapped himself in a burial shroud, laid himself in a coffin in his chamber, and prepared to increase his fortune.

But he had misjudged his servants, for when they heard the old skinflint was dead they unlocked the pantry and held a lavish party to celebrate. John Overs lay still for as long as he could. But eventually he could take it no more and, with a roar of anger, sat up to admonish his ungrateful employees. One of the servants took fright and, 'thinking the devil was rising' in his master's likeness, picked up an oar and 'struck out his brains'.

Although saddened at her father's tragic demise, Mary sent word to her lover that they could now be married, and he raced to plight his troth. But he was killed when his horse stumbled and threw him. Mary was now inundated with offers of marriage. But she chose instead to found the priory of St Mary Overies, and here lived out the remainder of her days. The priory has been Southwark Cathedral since 1905, and the interior is well worth exploring – especially the colourful Shakespeare Memorial Window.

The *Golden Hind*

Leave the cathedral and go right up the steps, then right along Cathedral Street. Follow the left fork in the road, which brings you to the replica of Sir Francis Drake's flagship, the *Golden Hind*. Feted as a hero in England, Drake was, not surprisingly, accused of all manner of foul deeds by his arch enemies, the Spanish, whose Armada he so devastatingly defeated in 1588. Rumour was rife that Drake had sold his soul to the Devil in exchange for prowess at sea, and that, in concert with Devon witches, he had cast spells to raise the storms that shattered the Spanish Armada. The replica is open to the public. On board, costumed guides will tell you all about 16th-century seafaring life, although talk of the Devil may be slightly frowned upon!

Leave foul winds, satanic pacts and the *Golden Hind* behind you and go straight ahead into Pickfords Wharf. On the left are the 14th-century remains of the Bishop of Winchester's Palace, a plaque on the rail details its history. Continue ahead into Clink Street where dark imposing Victorian warehouses rise cliff-like on either side.

There is little now to show of the days when cargoes from all over the world would have been offloaded into these storehouses. The lifting mechanisms hang eerily still, fastened onto walls where weeds and green shoots have sprouted from crevices and cracks in the crumbling brickwork, stained black by the soot from a hundred and more years of London fog and smogs. As the road narrows, a definite chill hangs in the air, and even on a bright summer's day long shadows line this section of road.

Clink Street is named for the Clink Prison, whose name has passed into popular usage, with a 'spell in clink' being the generic slang for a prison sentence. An exhibition of the gaol's history is located on the left.

The Smugglers of the Anchor Tavern

Continue onto Bankend, where you arrive at the Anchor Tavern. Situated on the banks of the Thames, this rambling, 18th-century pub was once a favoured haunt of

SOUTHWARK

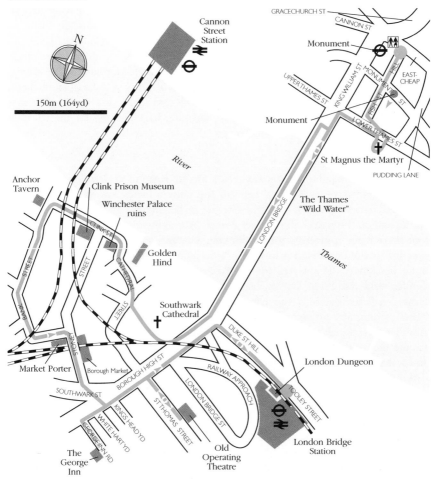

the writer Samuel Johnson – not to mention smugglers, who would hide their ill-gotten gains in secret rooms and cubby holes many of which only came to light during a major refurbishment in 1984. Sailors from the brigs and barges that had berthed on the river outside came here to refresh themselves. The press-gangs also came, to bribe, cajole or even kidnap 'volunteers' to crew the ships, and legend tells of one of the unfortunates dragged kicking and screaming from the pub. His cries for help were politely ignored by the other customers, who gazed into their tankards rather than risk attracting the attentions of the press men. But the customer's dog put up a spirited defence of its master, barking and snapping at the kidnappers, until one of the gang slammed the door shut with such force that it caught the animal's tail and cut it clean off. With a yelp of agonised pain, the dog ran into the night and was never seen again.

Times have changed and the docks are long gone. Today it is tourists, not sailors, who flock from the far-flung reaches of the globe to enjoy the hospitality of this wonderful old London landmark. The only press-gangs you are likely to encounter are groups of journalists from the nearby offices of the *Financial Times* and the *Daily Express*. But occasionally, as midnight approaches and the staff are clearing away the debris of another day's trading, there comes from nowhere the unmistakable sound of a dog's paws, padding along the corridors. Looking about them, some staff members have even seen the sad, dejected shade of a mangy dog as it wanders the warren of staircases, passages and snug bars, hunting for the tail it so tragically lost two and more centuries ago.

The Market Porter
Leave the Anchor and turn right along Park Street. Keep to the left side of the street and walk until you have passed beneath the railway bridge some distance along. The walk passes a modern council estate before becoming Victorian in appearance. At the end on the right is the Market Porter. Above the door in the pub's back parlour there hangs a hideous, sinister-looking African goat's head. Its gleaming glass eyes and twisted awkward grin lend it a decidedly demonic air as it scowls down upon customers. 'People tell me it attracts evil spirits,' the pub's landlord, Peter Conlan told the *South London Press*, 'but I don't believe in that sort of thing.' However, Peter was only too happy to acknowledge that his pub was haunted. 'After cashing up one night I awoke to find the upstairs till running all by itself... Another time the glass washer downstairs had been switched off and unplugged, but I came down the following morning to find it working with the door wide open and water flooding the bar... Neighbours have seen figures floating around in the darkness long after the last customer has left the pub.'

The George
Leave the Market Porter and turn right onto Stoney Street. Borough Market, London's oldest market, is to your left. Arrive at the traffic lights, cross over Southwark Street and continue across Borough High Street. Turn right off the crossing and go through the second gate on the left to find London's only surviving galleried coaching inn, the George, built in 1677.

Turning into the cobblestoned courtyard from the busy rush of Borough High Street, you find yourself transported back to another age. From the galleries that overhang the yard, long-forgotten travellers and inn workers once gazed down as the coaches clattered in through the gates. You can almost hear the whinnying of the horses, the cursing of the stablehands and the banter of the coachmen. You can imagine the passengers, stepping onto the stones, relieved that their journey was over or dreading its next leg.

It comes as little surprise to learn that this gem of bygone London is haunted. Several members of staff have woken in the early hours to find the misty form of a woman floating around their rooms. No one knows who she is, although a likely contender is the formidable Miss Murray, who kept the inn for fifty years in the later years of the last century and the beginning of this century. It was during her tenure that the railways sounded the death knell for the coaching age and led to the demolition of neighbouring inns. The new age of horseless transport meant that three galleries of her beloved George were demolished before public outcry succeeded in saving all that remained. Her spirit possesses outright antagonism towards modern technology. 'Anything electrical annoys the ghost,' says landlord, John Hall. 'New tills will always go wrong. We call the engineers but they can never find any logical explanation or genuine fault. Computers are the worst. It can take months of engineers coming and going before they will work properly, and even then they will suddenly crash for no apparent reason.'

Leave The George and turn right along Borough High Street, turning first right into St Thomas Street.

Florence Nightingale

Here you find the original site of St Thomas's Hospital where, in 1861, Florence Nightingale founded her School of Nursing. The hospital later moved from here to its present site in Lambeth. Parts of the old building still survive.

Go through the door of the brick church tower a little way along on the left. A winding wooden staircase with a rope banister twists its way upwards into the church's roof space, where the Old Operating Theatre can be found. This was opened in 1821, and is the oldest of its kind in the country. Huge glass jars containing pickled organs are balanced precariously on wooden display stands. Eager assistants are only too willing to don bloodstained aprons and demonstrate how operations were carried out in the days before anaesthesia, when the speed of the surgeon's blade was all that determined how much pain a patient would suffer.

Staff find working here late at night a spine-chilling experience. 'There's an atmosphere, especially in the Operating Theatre itself,' an assistant told me, 'and you do hear things.' Mike Barrell has worked here for over ten years, and has frequently heard footsteps climbing the stairs when the museum is closed and he has found himself alone here. On one occasion he and a colleague were tidying up after a late night function, when they both heard somebody running up the stairs towards a storeroom. Thinking a guest from the party had been left behind, they went to investigate but found the door locked fast and nobody else in the building.

There is a photograph on display in which, according to another assistant, 'lots of people can see the ghost of a nurse just standing in the background... some even think it is Florence Nightingale.'

Leave the Old Operating Theatre and return to Borough High Street. Turn right and then first right into the concourse of London Bridge Station, where the walk comes to an end. Should you wish to chill your marrow further, go past the station and then turn right into Tooley Street, where on the right, is located London's premier exhibition of horror, the London Dungeon, which boasts proudly, 'Enter at Your Peril.'

131

Greenwich

Location	5½ miles (8.8 kilometres) south-east of Charing Cross.
Transport	Greenwich Station (overground trains from Charing Cross and Cannon Street). Best Route Riverboats (from Charing Cross Pier or Tower Pier)
Refreshments	Numerous cafés, pubs and snack bars in Greenwich centre.

Greenwich is perhaps one of the most beautiful parts of London, and its lanes, river-front and park are a joy to explore and discover. Its hauntings are spread out, and so are here given as a sequence rather than a coherent walk. My suggestion is to follow them on the map, but take the time to explore everything else that Greenwich has to offer.

The best place to begin is on the riverside at the *Cutty Sark*. Nearby is the Royal Naval College, a superb complex of buildings mostly designed by Sir Christopher Wren, and formerly known as Greenwich Hospital. Behind this lies the National Maritime Museum, the oldest part of which is the Queen's House, designed by Inigo Jones for Anne of Denmark, the Consort of James I. Greenwich Park, rising beyond, provides views across East London. The old observatory, standing at the summit of the park's rolling grass hill, has a brass strip on the path outside that marks the zero meridian of longitude. Greenwich has much to see, and mingled among the illustrious array of ghosts that flit through it are all the other elements of a fascinating day out.

1. The *Cutty Sark*

Built in 1869, the *Cutty Sark* originally plied the China tea trade before making its name on the Australian woollen route. The fastest clipper of them all now stands marooned, its splendid figure-head gazing wistfully riverwise. The figurehead was intended as an emblem to protect the ship and all who sailed on her from the terrors of the deep.

Many tales tell of sailors on board the *Cutty Sark* seeing phantom ships. Whenever such a spectral image appeared the mariners would scuttle to the mast-head and, huddled beneath it, implore its protection.

A sailor new to the ship made himself extremely unpopular with his shipmates when he constructed a model of the figurehead in a bottle. All seamen knew that this object could only bring bad luck, and the mood on board became strained. One day a terrible storm blew up. Giant waves towered above the clipper as she tossed and pitched on the raging sea. Suddenly an enormous five-masted sailing ship appeared and hurtled towards them. The terrified sailors scurried to the figurehead and cowered beneath it, bracing themselves for the inevitable collision. A great wave rolled up and over them, smashing down onto the deck of the clipper, almost capsizing her. When the vessel righted itself the phantom ship had completely disappeared. The sailors later learned that, at the exact moment when the spectral boat had vanished, the sailor who had constructed the ship in a bottle had flung it into the wild and raging sea.

2. Elizabeth I Haunts the Royal Naval College

Standing on the site of Greenwich Palace, birthplace of Henry VIII, Mary I and Elizabeth I, the Royal Naval College dates from the latter half of the 17th century.

The palace had been a favourite residence of Elizabeth I, and her ghost returns from time to time to wander the grounds and buildings that have sprung up on the river bank. She wears a red wig and a low-necked period dress, but it is the small crown that adorns her hairpiece that has led to the conclusion it is indeed the shade of the virgin queen.

Admiral John Byng (1704–1757) haunts the rooms in the Queen Anne block where he was confined before being executed for neglect of duty. His footsteps are heard pacing back and forth in the room where he was imprisoned, and a shimmering apparition of him is often seen. The last occasion was on 15 June, 1993, when a security guard clearly saw him walk up the stairs of the Admiral President's Block at 11pm.

3. The Trafalgar Tavern

This roomy 19th-century hostelry, sitting proudly upon the banks of the Thames, in its time attracted the custom of the writers William Makepeace Thackeray, Wilkie Collins and Charles Dickens, the last of whom featured the tavern in *Little Dorrit*. Staff are agreed that there is a 'presence' at the pub, and that on occasion a distinct icy chill hangs in the air, while friends and family who come to stay often catch glimpses of a figure walking briskly across the upstairs rooms. When they turn to look closer it has disappeared without trace. The previous landlady treated the resident ghost as one would any house guest, and each morning would greet it. She was one of the few people never to be troubled by its activities. In early 1997 the bar manager, Douglas, saw the distinct figure of a man in Victorian dress sitting by the upstairs piano. Other staff have reported beer crates being lifted and moved around in the pub's cellars.

4. The Queen's House

In 1966 the Reverend and Mrs R. W. Hardy from White Rock, British Columbia, visited the Queen's House in Greenwich and took a photograph of the magnificent tulip staircase. When the film was duly developed upon their return to Canada, a shrouded figure was clearly visible on what had certainly been an empty staircase. Closer inspection revealed two ghostly figures, one wearing a ring a on the hand that gripped the banister as the two apparently ascended the tulip staircase. The photograph was brought to the attention of the Ghost Club, who asked experts at Kodak for their opinion. They ruled that the film had not been tampered with and there was no double exposure. They concluded that the only explanation for the appearance of the figures on the staircase was that they must have been there when the photograph was taken.

No one has ever explained who or what had appeared on the staircase, and subsequent attempts to repeat the phenomenon have proved futile. The phantom figures remain unexplained to this day. Perhaps this was a genuine spirit photograph of some long-forgotten residents making their weary way to bed.

5. Crooms Hill Gate, Greenwich Park

In 1934 a lady walking her dog by this gate was puzzled when the animal stopped in its tracks and began to growl, its hair standing on end. She saw a procession of ladies, all with reddish-brown hair and woollen clothes, carrying a heavy coffin upon their shoulders. Their legs stopped at the knees, giving the distinct impression that they were wading through the earth as though it were water. She watched dumbfounded as they walked slowly towards the gate, where they simply – vanished as mysteriously and as suddenly as they had appeared. The only explanation given for this remarkable and startling manifestation is the proximity of the gate to a series of barrows, the outlines of which are still clearly visible on the ground just inside the park. They were investigated in 1789 by a Reverend Douglas, who deemed them to represent a female burial ground dating from the 5th and 6th centuries. It was thought possible that the lady had seen a ghostly re-enactment of the funeral of one of these long-dead women, and that the raising of the ground since their time accounted for their missing legs.

6. The Jilted Lover of Hare and Billet Road

A doomed love affair accounts for the spectre that wanders dolefully along Hare and Billet Road. In the latter half of the 19th century a Greenwich woman of high birth fell in love with a married man. He promised her faithfully that he would leave his wife, and told her to meet him by a great elm that stood alongside a bleak and desolate stretch of road. He assured her that they would take a carriage and go abroad, where they could live happily together. But he never came and the heartbroken lady hanged herself from a branch of the elm, since when her shadowy form, in dark Victorian dress, has been seen here pacing anxiously back and forth, wringing her hands in despair as she waits in vain for her fickle lover to appear.

7. St John's Library

Formerly the vicarage of St John's Church, this was the childhood home of Elsie Marshall, whose father became vicar in 1874. Elsie became a missionary and in 1892 set sail for China to spread the good word in a remote province. Her cheerful and patient countenance inspired all who met her. On 1 August, 1895, a gang of bandits attacked the mission and slaughtered everyone, including poor Elsie Marshall. Her spirit journeyed back to the house in which she had grown up and now the library staff have grown quite fond of Elsie's ghost, who harms no one as she makes her presence known in a variety of mischievous ways, including switching on all the lights when the building is empty. One or two visitors to the library have been slightly dis-

GREENWICH

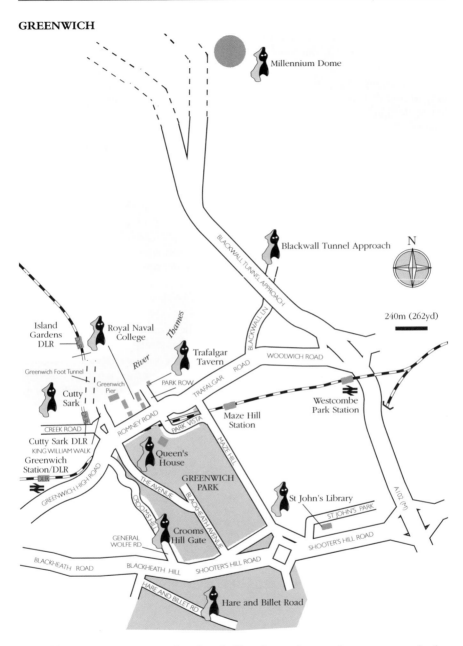

turbed by an unseen presence that they feel brush past them at the entrance, and others have felt a cold touch on the back of their necks, but when they learn that it is the harmless, inoffensive ghost of tragic Elsie Marshall they simply smile and feel quite honoured to have been singled out for her ethereal attention.

8. The Blackwall Tunnel

In October 1972 a motor cyclist stopped to pick up a male hitchhiker on the Greenwich approach to the tunnel. On the journey through the tunnel, the two managed to hold a conversation, during which the man told the driver where he lived. Emerging from the tunnel, the motor cyclist turned to make a comment, only to find that the man had vanished. He drove several times through the tunnel but could find no sign of his passenger.

Mystified, he went round to the address he had been given, and was told that the description he gave matched that of the son of the family, who had been dead for many years.

9. The Millennium Dome

The site now occupied by the Millennium Dome was formerly home to the South Metropolitan Gas Works, the offices of which were long rumoured to be haunted. It was widely believed that the bearded phantom, who made frequent appearances and wreaked havoc by messing up the desks of alarmed employees, was the ghost of the company's former chairman, Sir George Livesey. When he was alive,Livesey introduced a profit-sharing scheme for the workers and made a lasting impression as a philanthropist. He was so popular that, when he died 90 years ago, over 7,000 people attended his funeral.

Once the Gas Works had closed down, the ghost was often seen roaming the derelict site, and it was rumoured that its visits increased dramatically when workers began to construct the Millennium Dome. As the workers raced to complete the dome by the year 2000, Livesey's distinguished figure materialised before them and let loose long peals of chuckling laughter. Spokespersons for the Millennium project were forced to confess bafflement as to what could be causing the spectre such obvious merriment.

Plate 27: *The imposing gates of Old Scotland Yard, the former headquarters of the Metropolitan Police, shown in an early lantern slide. The old Yard's Black Museum of Crime Memorabilia was once haunted by a hooded but headless lady (see page 103).*

Plate 28: *The Horseguards Building in Whitehall. A precognitive dream only just prevented the coronation of Edward VII coming to an abrupt halt beneath the central arch (see page 103).*

Plate 29: *This famous image shows Cleopatra's Needle on Victoria Embankment. At this site a laughing naked figure is said to entice passers-by to a watery grave (see page 114).*

Plate 30: *The Savoy Hotel, home of Kaspar the wooden cat (see page 114).*

Plate 31: *Ye Olde Cheshire Cheese tavern in Wine Office Court (see page 117).*

Plate 32: *St Paul's Cathedral where a ghostly white-haired cleric tunelessly whistles his way to a secret doorway (see page 122).*

Plate 33: With its cobbled alleyways, historic observatory and naval heritage, the old London 'village' of Greenwich contains many haunted sites (see page 132).

Plate 34: A carved detail in Southwark Cathedral (see page 127) reminds all who pass by of what the future ultimately holds.

Plate 35: At Pluckley, England's most haunted village, both the 'Red Lady' and the 'White Lady' haunt the churchyard of St Nicholas's church (see page 138).

Pluckley: England's Most Haunted Village

Transportation	Overground trains from Charing Cross and London Bridge stations. (journey time just over one hour) For buses from the railway station to the village Tel: 0345-696996
Start	St Nicholas's Church, The Street
Finish	The Black Horse Inn, The Street
Distance	4 miles (6.4 kilometres)
Duration	2 hours
Best Time	During the day, when the magnificent village church is open and when the picturesque countryside can be best appreciated.
Refreshments	The Black Horse Inn and the Blacksmith's Tea Rooms are both passed on the walk.

Pluckley nestles in the lush Kent countryside just a short drive away from London. I have included it not only for its reputation as the most haunted village in England but also because it is a pretty, picturesque place which might be familiar as the setting for the recent television series *The Darling Buds of May*. There are a number of spots around the village that have a distinctive feel to them, and several of these haunted places are connected to the Dering family, lords of the manor from the 15th century until World War I. An intriguing remnant of their tenure can be seen in the round-topped windows that grace so many of the buildings. During the Civil War, Lord Dering escaped capture by Cromwell's forces when he dived head-first through such a window. When he later came to rebuild his manor house he commemorated the feat by having every window built in the same style, and this in turn was copied throughout the village. Sadly, the house itself burnt down in 1951, but many houses you pass on the walk still feature this reminder of his great escape.

The walk will give you the chance to enjoy picturesque countryside and fresh, pure air, albeit air charged with a great deal of psychic energy!

The Ghosts of St Nicholas's Church

Located at the top of the first aisle in St Nicholas's Church is the Dering Chapel, where numerous members of the family lie buried. A strange, dancing light has frequently been seen in the upper section of the window to your right. It is often accompanied by the sound of knocking coming from the family vault beneath your feet.

In the early 1970s, in the hope of recording supernatural phenomena, a group of psychic researchers persuaded the rector, the Reverend John Pittock, to allow them to spend a night locked inside the church. Armed with their cameras, tape

PLUCKLEY

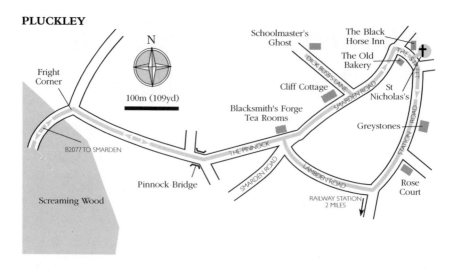

recorders, thermometers and other apparatus, they settled down to watch and wait. When the vicar came to let them out the next morning they complained of having spent an uneventful night, the boredom of which had been alleviated only by the vicar's dog, who had come to visit them from time to time. 'Actually,' the vicar commented, 'I don't have a dog.'

Leave the church and go ahead along the pathway. Listen carefully as you move between the gravestones for the voice of the 'Red Lady'. She is reputed to have been a member of the Dering clan whose baby died at birth and was buried in an unmarked grave, possibly because it was illegitimate. She herself died shortly afterwards, some say of a broken heart, and was laid in the family vault. But her apparition, in a flowing red dress, often appears in the churchyard, drifting silently between the tombstones, calling to her lost child.

She shares her weary search with another female member of the Dering family, the 'White Lady'. This woman's beauty was famed throughout the neighbourhood, and when she died, at a tragically young age, her husband was grief-stricken. He could not bear the thought of the effect that the ravages of the grave would have upon her looks, so he had her body wrapped in a priceless flowing gown. She was placed in an airtight lead coffin with a single red rose laid upon her breast. Sealed inside a further series of airtight lead coffins, she was finally encased in a casket of solid oak and buried in a deep vault in the Dering Chapel. But on misty autumn mornings she breaks free from these confines and manifests in the churchyard, as beautiful in death as she was in life. Her flowing black hair is a striking contrast to the white of her gown. Clutched before her she holds a single red rose.

Greystones – A Monkly Haunt

On arrival at the church gate pass out onto The Street. Follow the road as it forks left and becomes Station Road. Keep ahead until, on the left, you arrive at the large white house.

This house, Greystones, is haunted by a monk who drifts among the surrounding trees. He is said to have lived in Tudor times, and is reputed to have fallen in love with the daughter of a neighbouring property. As we shall see shortly (see below), she died under tragic circumstances and he sank into a state of melancholy and bitterness. His only solace was to walk the green fields and leafy lanes where they had enjoyed so many romantic interludes together. But, as time passed, he sank deeper into depression, pining for his dead lover, and finally died of a broken heart. His ghost, however, continued to wander the neighbourhood, and was last seen in 1989 by an American journalist who glimpsed his unmistakable brown-robed figure drifting behind the house.

Proceed along Station Road and try to sense the feeling that is said to pervade this section. More than one person walking along here has heard the sound of a man and woman chatting happily, accompanied by a dog's playful yapping. Closer and closer they get until they are virtually upon you, and then the phantoms fade as they pass along the road – much as they have done for as long as anyone can remember.

Rose Court and an Anachronistic Tale

A little further along you arrive at an unnamed road that stretches away to the left. Behind the hedge on the right of this can be seen Rose Court. The house is at least 250 years old, and is said to have been built by a member of the Dering family for his mistress; there is no exact date, but the period is generally described as Tudor. Whatever the case, the story goes that she fell in love with the monk who lived at Greystones (see above), and found the love triangle so distressing that she drank a fatal cocktail distilled from the juices of ivy and other poisonous berries. When her body was discovered, it was apparent that her final moments had been spent looking across the field to Greystones. The fact that Greystones wasn't built until 1863 – should not stand in the way of a perfectly good ghost story, there could have been another house on the site then! Strange things do indeed happen within Rose Court. Articles are moved around in the night, strange groans and sighs disturb the early hours and it is said that a peculiar eerie atmosphere hangs over the garden.

Move along Station Road and take the next turning right into Lambden Road, which is lined with houses that span many ages and include a few tasteful barn conversions. At the end of the road turn right, then go first left, just before the Blacksmith's Tea Rooms, into The Pinnock. There now follows a long walk made worthwhile by the stunning view across the countryside to your right.

Just past where a road signposted Smarden and Bethesden, goes to the left, you arrive at Pinnock Bridge, an easily missed stone bridge that passes over a tiny, babbling brook. On its banks, earlier this century, an old gypsy lady eked out a meagre living gathering watercress and selling it to the villagers. She was a well known local character, considered eccentric but harmless. Each night as the sun went down she would sit on the walls of this bridge, smoke her clay pipe and drink gin from a battered old flask. One evening she fell asleep. The pipe dropped onto the rags she wore for clothing, and within moments she had erupted into a raging ball of flame. No one heard her agonised screams. She was found the next day, a charred pile of ashes, the battered old flask and the shattered clay pipe lying nearby.

But her ghost has been seen many times since. In the years that followed her tragic death, she manifested as a screaming, howling figure surrounded by flame. But in latter years she has become nothing more than a faint, pink glow, that hovers in the air on the spot where the 'Watercress Lady' was burnt to death.

Fright Corner and Screaming Wood

At the end of The Pinnock you arrive at a crossroads, where signposts point every way. This is the aptly named Fright Corner. A highwayman is said to have met a gruesome end here. He was pursued across the fields by the forces of law and order, and made his last stand with his back to an oak tree that stood here until quite recently. He put up a tremendous and spirited fight, but was finally overpowered and run through with the cold sharp steel of several swords. His last desperate battle is, from time to time, repeated before startled witnesses who pass this spot in the early hours of winter evenings. Others see his lifeless body, slumped forwards and pinned to a phantom tree by a large sword that protrudes from his chest.

Take the road marked 'Smarden'. About a hundred yards along on the left is the entrance to what is officially known as Dering Wood but is locally nicknamed Screaming Wood. It is an eerie experience to walk these muddy paths through the skeletal trees, especially when it is getting dark. The journey is made even spookier by the knowledge that many lone wayfarers who have come this way have been scared witless by a sudden loud, anguished scream. It comes from deep within the wood and sends the birds flapping from the trees.

The Blacksmith's Forge Tea Rooms

Dally in Screaming Wood for as long as you dare, then return to Fright Corner. Backtrack along The Pinnock. At the end on the left is the tea room. The building's origins go back to the 14th century, when it housed a blacksmith's forge. It then became an alehouse, but it is now a charming, cosy tea room run by Gloria Atkins, who shares her home with at least two ghosts. One is a cavalier whose jovial form has been seen by several members of the family striding in and out of various upstairs rooms. The other is a Tudor maid, who stands by the fireplace slowly turning the spit, watched by bemused customers.

Gloria has experienced further phenomena, such as a line of hanging mugs suddenly clinking together as though someone had just walked by and run a finger along them. On a cold November afternoon in 1997, as she was working in the kitchen, she heard the front door open and close. This was followed by the sound of a chair being moved away from a table. Picking up her notepad, she went to take the customer's order only to find that the tea room was empty. She could see that a chair had been moved back from the table, but there was nobody in the building.

Go left from the tea room and along Smarden Road. Continue for quite a distance along a section of road that is lined with houses at certain spots and is quite remote at others. On arrival at Cliff Cottage, turn left into the uneven and unpaved Dick Buss's Lane, named for a 1930s miller whose premises were reached by this tree-lined thoroughfare.

In the 1920s, at the end of this lane, a group of children on their way to school came upon the body of their teacher, hanging from the branch of a tree. The reason for his suicide was never discovered, but on certain nights, when a light breeze rustles the trees and a full moon sits high over the neighbourhood, his ghostly form is clearly seen, swinging back and forth, hanging from the branch where his living form breathed its anguished last.

The Old Bakery and a Phantom Coach

Return to Smarden Road, turn left, go up the hill and then turn right onto The Street, where the first building on the right is the bakery. Renovation to this property included the removal of an old Victorian fireplace, and this exposed the original hearth. This prompted a spate of inexplicable happenings, including ghostly footsteps that stamped across an upper room and fell silent as they reached the fireplace. Residents reported an icy chill hanging in the air at this spot on even the hottest day. This section of the road is apparently the route used by a phantom coach and spectral horses that are heard, but never seen, racing by the houses in the early hours of the morning.

A Spectral Prankster in the Black Horse Inn

Go a little further along The Street and on the left you will find the Black Horse Inn. This delightful, atmospheric hostelry was built in the 14th century as a farmhouse, at which time it was encircled by a deep moat, long since filled in although still discernible in places. The pub is haunted by a ghostly prankster who delights in hiding the personal possessions of staff and customers alike, and who has locked the landlady out of her pub on more than one occasion.

Laura Gambling took over the pub in November 1997 and on her first Sunday was enjoying a cup of tea just prior to opening for the busy Sunday lunchtime session. She noticed a glass on the shelf above the bar move just a little. As she watched it she was astonished when it began to slide along the length of the shelf, stopping when it reached the edge. Other ghostly activity includes: an unseen hand that lifts cutlery from the dresser and arranges it neatly on the side; a spot in the kitchen where the pet dogs stop abruptly and bark at something, or someone, that only they can see; and an upstairs room that the dogs refuse to enter and where Laura's twelve-year-old daughter has seen a 'nice lady in a red dress'. Indeed, so haunted is this delightful and cosy old pub that it makes the ideal place to relax and unwind at the end of your perambulation around England's most haunted village.

141

A Gaggle of Ghosts

This chapter describes a selection of interesting haunted places that would not fit into any grouping of ghostly sites. In each case I have given the address and the nearest Underground station. Opening times and details of any admission charges are dealt with in the section headed Further Information (see pages 148–53).

Westminster Abbey
Nearest Underground Station: Westminster (Circle and District lines)
In the 6th century the area of Westminster was an inhospitable island that rose from the marshy banks of the Thames where it was joined by the Tyburn Stream.

It was here that the newly converted king of the East Saxons, Serbert, built a church dedicated to St Peter and consecrated by Mellitus, the first Bishop of London. Legend tells that, on the night before the consecration, a cloaked stranger appeared on the south side of the river and asked a fisherman to row him across. As the tiny vessel reached the opposite bank, the fisherman watched in amazement as the church suddenly glowed with a brilliance that illuminated the night sky and the air was filled with singing angels. The mysterious passenger revealed himself to be St Peter, and then anointed the walls with holy water and proceeded to dedicate his own church.

For nearly five hundred years afterwards the Benedictine Monastery of St Peter flourished on the site, and then Edward the Confessor rebuilt it. A few days after its consecration in January 1066, the saintly Edward died, being buried in front of the high altar. Not long afterwards King Harold was crowned there, but before the year was out he had been killed at the battle of Hastings. The days of the Saxons were over, and William I was crowned King in the Abbey on Christmas Day. The Norman rule had begun, and with it the tradition of crowning the English sovereign in the Abbey.

The Abbey has been considerably altered, the last major addition being the construction of Henry VII's Chapel in 1503. During modifications the floor level was progressively lowered by a good two feet, which may be why the ghostly monk, often seen around the Abbey appears to float a significant distance above the ground. In 1932 this spectral cleric actually held a conversation with two American visitors, who found him pleasant and quite revealing about his past. But his major performance has to be his 1900 appearance, when he kept visitors entertained for a good twenty-five minutes before walking backwards and vanishing into a wall of the cloisters.

The Tomb of the Unknown Warrior is a poignant memorial to those who gave their lives in World War I. Brought to England on 11 November, 1920, the complete though unidentified body was given a royal funeral and buried in soil gathered from the battlefields of France, beneath a marble stone quarried in Belgium. From time to time, when the crowds have gone and the Abbey settles into a peaceful and quiet stillness, a ghostly soldier materialises by the tomb and stands for a few moments, his head bowed in sorrow, gazing contemplatively upon the tomb where his earthly remains lie in an unnamed grave.

St Giles Cripplegate

Nearest Underground Station: Barbican (Circle and District lines)

The following story probably falls into the category of urban myth, and almost identical versions are repeated all over the country.

A shoemaker's wife living in the parish died and, in keeping with the wishes of her heartbroken husband, was buried in the crypt of St Giles wearing her wedding dress and wedding ring upon her finger. At midnight the sexton returned to the church, removed the lid from the lady's coffin and, by flickering lanternlight, attempted to remove the ring. No matter how hard he pulled the ring would not come off, so he took his pocket knife and proceeded to slice through her finger. Her eyes opened wide and she let out a blood-curdling scream and sat bolt upright in her coffin. The sexton took fright and ran from the church, leaving the poor lady to come to her senses.

At length she staggered from the coffin, picked up the discarded lantern and, holding it before her, walked home and knocked upon the door. A maidservant came down, opened the door, screamed out, slammed the door in her mistress's face and went running to the master, convinced that his wife's ghost had come to take their souls. He went to the door, brought his wife in, and put her to bed with a warm drink. She lived for many more years, had four more children and became known as the 'Cripplegate Ghost'.

Aldgate Underground Station

Working alone in an Underground station can be an eerie experience, and Aldgate, situated at a convergence of rail lines to the east of the city, is no exception. In the 1950s a station foreman happened to glance over at an electrician who was carrying out essential maintenance on the rail tracks and was surprised to see a grey-haired old lady stroking the man's hair. Moments later the colleague made a potentially fatal error that sent 22,000 volts surging through his body. Despite being knocked unconscious, he suffered no other ill effects, and was ever afterwards grateful to the guardian angel whose touch he was sure had saved his life.

Inexplicable happenings are so frequent at Aldgate that a station log is kept in which they are recorded. Entries include reference to the sound of echoing footsteps across the sleepers, often accompanied by cheerful whistling as though some contented railman from days gone by were carrying out a track inspection.

Bruce Castle, Lordship Lane, N17

Nearest Main Line Station: Bruce Grove (trains from Liverpool St)

This is an Elizabethan manor house, and local tradition holds that it stands on the

143

site of a castle built by King Robert the Bruce's father, the manor belonging to the Scottish royal family until the 14th century.

Looking above the entrance porch and above the clock you will see the windows of a small chamber. It was here that Lord Coleraine is said to have imprisoned his beautiful wife, Constantia, for fear that anyone else should gaze upon her. On 3 November, 1680 she picked up her baby, walked to the window and threw herself to her death from the balustrade. Her terrifying screams were heard each year on the anniversary until, earlier this century, a sympathetic clergyman took pity on her and held a prayer service in the room. It quelled the screams but her silent form is still occasionally seen repeating her suicide.

In July 1971 two people walking past the building late one night saw a group of people in 18th-century costume apparently enjoying a ball. What caught their attention was that they made no sound and appeared to be floating around the festivities. Another couple saw the figures a few days later and this time approached them, whereupon one by one the figures slowly melted into the walls of the building.

Bruce Castle was formerly the home of postal reformer Sir Rowland Hill (1795–1879), who devised the Penny Post, and today it houses a postal and local history museum.

St Mary's Church, Neasden Lane/Eric Road, NW10

Nearest Underground Station: Neasden (Jubilee Line)
The south aisle of the church is believed to be of the 13th century whereas the nave is a 19th-century rebuilding. The church is haunted by an unseen priest who is said to create a bit of a nuisance. The mysterious odour of incense is frequently smelt by parishioners and visitors alike, and the rattling door handle in the vestry is a constant source of irritation to those working alone in the church. The grounds of the church are haunted by a jovial monk in black robes who has been seen prowling around at all hours of the day.

Richmond Palace

Nearest Station: Richmond (District Line and Main Line station)
In January 1603, the astrologer Dr John Dee cast the horoscope of Queen Elizabeth I and advised her to leave Whitehall Palace for Richmond Palace. Little now survives of the old Palace, save a courtyard and the red-brick gatehouse, but in 1603 it was nown as Elizabeth's 'warm winter box'. In mid-February, her close friend and cousin the Countess of Nottingham died, plunging the ageing Queen into a severe depression. By 11 March, she had succumbed to a severe chill which soon turned into pneumonia and it was apparent that the Queen was dangerously ill. However, she refused to be taken to her bed, claiming that 'If you were in the habit of seeing such things in your bed as I do when in mine, you would not persuade me to go there.'

Ten days later it was obvious to all that the Queen was dying, and only then did she take to her bed. At around 10 o'clock on the night of 23 March, the old Queen sighed, turned her face to the wall, and sank into a deep sleep. As she did so, one of her ladies-in-waiting left the room to return briefly to her own quarters. As she hurried along one of the gloomy corridors, she was astonished to see the unmistakable figure of the Queen striding purposefully towards her. She briefly looked away and by the time she looked again the figure had vanished. In a state of bemused agitation, the lady rushed back to the bedchamber only to find Elizabeth still unconscious, just as she had left her a few minutes before. It would appear that as the last of the Tudor monarchs clung desperately to life, her spirit had somehow left her body to wander the corridors of Richmond Palace one last time.

Hall Place, Bourne Road, Bexley, Kent

Nearest Main Line Station: Bexley (trains from Charing Cross)
This flint-and-brick Tudor house, with a 17th-century addition, is named for the 13th-century owners of the property, the At-Halls. It was from here in 1346 that Edward III's eldest son, better known as the Black Prince, set off to fight in the French campaign. His phantom returns here and is considered a bad omen for the fortunes of England. Clad in black armour and accompanied by the occasional chords of medieval music, he is said to have appeared three times prior to British setbacks during World War II.

Hall Place's second ghost is thought to be that of Lady Constance At-Hall, who witnessed her husband, Sir Thomas, being killed by a stag and threw herself to her death from the tower. Her pitiful moans are said to drift through the house, mysterious footsteps and strange tappings are heard in the night and, every so often, a shadowy figure is seen on the tower. In the 1950s a medium visited the house and established that some of the crying is caused by a servant girl who suffered personal tragedy and whose wraith is now seen in one of the attic bedrooms.

The Old Palace, Croydon

Nearest Main Line Station: East Croydon or West Croydon (trains from Victoria)
Now a school, this was formerly the home of successive archbishops of Canterbury, the medieval lords of the manor. It was visited by many illustrious figures, including Henry III, Edward I, Henry IV, Henry VII, Henry VIII, Mary I and Elizabeth I. James I of Scotland was held prisoner here before becoming King. The archbishops moved out in 1758 after nearly 750 years of occupation and the building later became a school for lost orphans. The ghost that haunts the Old Palace is that of the mother of one of the 19th-century children. She appears terribly sad, wringing her hands in grief as she wanders the building in search of her lost child.

Barnes Common, Common Road, London SW13

Nearest Main Line Station: Barnes (trains from Waterloo)
Little now remains of the original Common, which in 1838 was one site of the infamous haunting by 'Spring Heel Jack'. He came bounding from the vicinity of the old churchyard, his appearance 'hideous and frightful... vomiting blue and white flame from his mouth', and attacked lone wayfarers who found themselves alone on the Common at night. After a short reign of terror, his appearances ceased as abruptly as they had begun.

These days the Common is haunted by the wraith of a man in grey prison clothes who glides furtively around looking as though he is about to commit a crime. One theory is that he is the ghost of a 19th-century convict who, having escaped from nearby Putney Hospital, froze to death on the Common.

The Royal Stag Pub, The Green, Datchet, Berks

Nearest Main Line Station: Datchet (trains from Waterloo)

The picturesque village of Datchet is just a short distance from Windsor. On a corner next to the church sits this cosy old pub where, from time to time, a spectral handprint suddenly becomes visible on one of the windows. The story goes that, in a deep 19th-century midwinter, a labourer came to the pub and made his young son wait outside while he drank his ale inside. The boy made his way round to the graveyard immediately next door and tried to keep warm. But it was bitterly cold and he eventually walked to the window of the pub and tried to attract his father's attention. The man ignored the lad, who, in a last act of desperation, pressed his hand hard against the windowpane, then slipped exhausted into the snow and froze to death. Ever since that long-ago day, his ghostly handprint has occasionally appeared on the pane. In 1979 a national newspaper featured the story and employed a local glazier to remove the glass so that it could be subjected to scientific analysis. The technicians were forced to admit that it was nothing more than an ordinary piece of very old glass. Meanwhile, the handprint had appeared on the replacement pane that had been fitted in its place.

A photograph of the handprint is on show inside the pub. It is a clear imprint of a small left palm, fingers and thumb, without doubt those of a young child.

Acknowledgements

Numerous people and organisations have helped me with the research and the writing of this book. Staff at local libraries have helped me trace haunted sites in their area, and special mention must go to the staff at the excellent Guildhall Library. I would like to thank Tom and Stacey Lang of the New Orleans Vampire Tour for their invaluable assistance and for providing me with their research notes on Dracula. I have met people who have shared their ghostly tales, or directed me to haunted buildings, while to others I was just a voice on the end of a telephone checking the latest details of their hauntings. I would like to say a special thank you to those who patiently and willingly answered my questions.

Among friends and family I offer my heartfelt thanks to my wife Joanne, for listening as I tested out my ghost stories for their spooky effect, a service that was certainly not mentioned in our marriage vows! My special thanks go to Geraldine Hennigan and Rosaleen Ciavucco, who read my stories and proffered useful suggestions; Jonathan Unwin, who rescued numerous records despite my computer illiteracy; and Paul Roberts, who helped with testing the routes.

Last but by no means least, I thank all those who have gone before, whose ghostly hauntings have made this book possible. May you rest in peace.

Richard Jones

Further Information

Opening times

Opening times often change at short notice so, where applicable, telephone numbers are included. Pubs, unless listed here, are open daily at the normal hours of 11.00–23.00.

1. The Tower of London, Tower Hill EC3 Tel: 0207-709 0765
Mar–Oct: Mon–Sat 9.00–17.00, Sun 10.00–17.00. Oct–Mar: Tue–Sat 9.00–16.00, Sun and Mon 10.00–16.00. Admission charge.

2. Alleyways of the Old City
St Botolph's, Bishopsgate EC2
Mon–Fri 10.00–16.00.
The George and Vulture, 3 Castle Court EC3 Tel: 0207-626 9710
Mon–Fri 12.00–14.45.
The Bank of England Museum, Threadneedle Street EC2 Tel: 0207-601 5545
Mon–Fri 10.00–17.00.
St Mary-le-Bow Church, Cheapside EC2
Mon–Fri 8.30–17.30 (closes at 16.00 during August).
Williamson's Tavern, Groveland Court EC2 Tel: 0207-248 6280
Mon–Fri 11.00–23.00.
St James Garlick Hythe Church, Garlick Hill EC2
Mon–Fri 10.00–16.00.

3. The City of the Dead
Central Criminal Courts, Old Bailey EC1 Tel: 0207-248 3277
Courts open Mon–Fri 10.00–16.00 (with adjournment for lunch). No cameras are allowed inside the building.
The Viaduct Tavern, 126 Newgate Street EC1 Tel: 0207-606 8476
Seven days a week 11.00–23.00.
St Bartholomew-the-Great Church, Cloth Fair EC1
Mon–Thurs and Sat 8.00–16.30, Fri 10.30–16.00, Sun 8.00–16.00.
Ye Old Red Cow, Long Lane EC1
Mon–Fri 11.00–23.00.

4. Clerkenwell
Charterhouse, Charterhouse Square EC1 Tel: 0207-253 9503
Guided Tours take place at 14.15 April–July.
St John's Gate Museum, St John's Lane Clerkenwell EC1 Tel: 0207-253 6644
Mon–Fri 10.00–17.00, Sat 10.00–16.00.
Tours of 1½ hours duration take place on Tue, Fri and Sat at 11.00 and 14.30.

Clerks Well, 16 Farringdon Lane EC1   Tel: 0207-689 7960

5. Lincoln's Inn Fields to Bloomsbury
The Ship Tavern, Gate Street WC1
Mon–Fri 11.00–23.00.
Lincoln's Inn WC1
Mon–Fri 9.00–18.00.
The Dolphin Pub, Red Lion Street WC1
Mon–Sat 11.00–23.00.
The British Museum, Great Russell Street WC1   Tel: 0207-636 1555
Mon–Sat 10.00–17.00, Sun 14.30–18.00.
The Atlantis Bookshop, 49a Museum Street WC1   Tel: 0207-405 2120
Mon–Sat 11.00–18.00.

6. Highgate
Highgate Cemetery, Swains Lane N6   Tel: 0208-340 1834
Eastern cemetery open Apr–Oct: Mon–Fri 10.00–17.00, Sat and Sun
11.00–17.00. Nov–Mar: Mon–Fri 10.00–16.00, Sat and Sun 11.00–16.00.
Western cemetery: can be visited only on guided tours Apr–Oct: Mon–Fri 12.00,
14.00 and 16.00; Sat and Sun on the hour, every hour 11.00–16.00. Nov and
Mar same as above except last tour departs 15.00. Dec–Feb: Sat and Sun only on
the hour every hour 11.00–15.00. Both cemeteries are closed during
funerals. Admission charge.
Lauderdale House, Waterlow Park, Highgate Hill N6   Tel: 0208-348 8716
Tue–Fri 11.00–16.00.

7. Hampstead
St John's Church, Church Row NW3
Seven days a week 9.00–17.00.
The Holly Bush, 22 Holly Mount NW3   Tel: 0207-435 2892
Mon–Fri 12.00–15.00, 17.30–23.00; Sat 12.00–23.00; Sun 12.00–22.30.
Fenton House, Hampstead Grove NW3   Tel: 0207-435 3471
Mar: Sat and Sun 14.00–17.00. Apr–Oct: Sat and Sun 11.00–17.00, Wed, Thur
and Fri 14.00–17.30.
Spaniards Inn, Spaniards Lane NW3   Tel: 0208-731 6571
Mon–Sat 11.00–23.00, Sun 12.00–22.30.

8. Enfield
Rose and Crown, Clay Hill   Tel: 0208-363 2010
Mon–Sat 11.00–23.00, Sun 12.00–22.30.

9. Great Portland Street to Theatreland
BBC Experience, Portland Place W1   Tel: 0870 6030304
Mon 13.00–16.30, Tue–Fri 9.30–16.30, Sat and Sun 9.30–17.30. Admission charge.
London Palladium, Argyll Street W1   Tel: 0207-494 5020

Theatre tours Mon–Sat 12.30 and 16.30.
Burlington Arcade, Piccadilly W1 Mon–Sat 10.00–18.00.
Theatre Royal, Haymarket SW1 Tel: 0207-930 8890
Theatre tours available but phone for details.

10. Royal London
Golden Lion, 25 King Street SW1 Tel: 0207-930 7227.

11. Belgravia and Chelsea
Apsley House, Wellington Museum, 149 Piccadilly W1 Tel: 0207-499 5676
Tue–Sun 11.00–17.00. Admission charge.
Spiritualist Association, 33 Belgrave Square SW1 Tel: 0207-235 3351
Medium demonstrations take place Mon–Fri 15.30 and 19.00, Sat 16.00, Sun 18.00. Admission charge.

12. Kensington to Notting Hill
Kensington Palace, Kensington Gardens W8 Tel: 0207-937 9561. Admission charge. Summer 10.00–18.00. Phone for winter openings.

13. Chiswick
Chiswick House and Grounds, Burlington Lane W4 Tel: 0208-995 0508
Apr–Sep seven days a week 10.00–13.00 and 14.00–18.00. Oct–Mar: Wed–Sun 10.00–13.00 and 14.00–16.00. Admission charge.
St Nicholas's Church, Church Street W4. Sun 14.30–17.00.

14. Wimbledon
Wimbledon Theatre, The Broadway SW19 Tel: 0208-540 0362.

15. *Hampton Court Palace*, East Molesey, Surrey Tel: 0208-781 9500
Apr–Oct: Mon 10.15–18.00, Tue–Sun 9.30–18.00. Oct–Mar: Mon 10.15–16.30, Tue–Sun 9.30–16.30. Admission charge.

16. Windsor and Eton
Windsor Castle, Windsor, Berks Tel: 01753 743900
Seven days a week 10.00–16.00, last admission 15.00. Admission charge.
Eton College, Eton, Berks Tel: 01753 671000
Mar–Oct: daily during term time 14.00–16.30, out of term time 10.30–16.30.

17. Westminster to Piccadilly
Banqueting House, Whitehall WC2 Tel: 0207-930 4179
Mon–Sat 10.00–17.00, last admission 16.30. Times may change due to functions so phone for details. Admission charge.
Gordon's Wine Bar, Villiers Street WC2 Tel: 0207-930 1408
Mon–Fri 11.00–23.00, Sat 17.00–23.00.
Davenports Magic, 5–7 Charing Cross Underground Arcade, WC2 Tel: 0207-836 0408
Mon–Fri 9.30–17.30, Sat 10.15–16.00.

18. Covent Garden
St Paul's Church, Bedford Street WC2
Mon–Fri 9.00–16.00.
Rules Restaurant, 35 Maiden Lane WC2 Tel: 0207-836 5314
Seven days a week midday to midnight.
Theatre Royal, Drury Lane WC2 Tel: 0207-494 5091
Backstage tours. Mon, Tue, Thurs and Fri 10.30, 13.00, 14.30 and 17.30; Wed and
Sat 10.30 and 12.30; Sun 12.00, 14.00 and 15.30.
Somerset House, Strand WC2 Tel: 0207-936 6000
Mon–Sat 10.00–18.00, Sun 14.00–18.00.

19. Gaslit Ghosts, the Temple and Fleet Street
Middle Temple Dining Hall, Middle Temple Lane EC4
Closed to the public but a polite enquiry at the office, weekdays before midday, can
often get you admitted.
Temple Church, Pump Court EC4
Wed–Sun 10.00–16.00.
Ye Olde Cheshire Cheese, Wine Office Court EC4 Tel: 0207-353 6170
Mon–Fri 11.30–23.00, Sat 11.30–15.00 and 17.30–23.00, Sun 12.00–16.00.
Royal Courts of Justice, Strand WC2
Mon–Fri 10.00–16.00. No cameras are allowed inside the building.

20. The Blackfriars Walk
The Blackfriar Pub, 174 Queen Victoria Street EC4 Tel: 0207-236 5650
Mon–Fri 11.30–23.00.
St Andrew by the Wardrobe, Queen Victoria Street EC4
Mon–Fri 8.00–16.00.
St Paul's Cathedral, St Paul's Churchyard EC4 Tel: 0207-236 4128
Mon–Sat 8.30–16.00. Sun services only. There is an admission charge but the
haunted Kitchener Chapel can be viewed without paying.

21. Southwark
St Magnus the Martyr Church, Lower Thames Street EC3
Mon–Fri 10.00–16.00.
Southwark Cathedral, Borough High Street SE1
Seven days a week 10.00–16.00.
Golden Hind, St Mary Overie Dock, Cathedral Street SE1 Tel: 0207-403 0123
Seven days a week 10.00–17.00 (sometimes closed at weekends for weddings and
birthday parties).
The Clink Prison Museum, Clink Street SE1 Tel: 0207-403 6515
Seven days a week 10.00–18.00. Admission charge.
The Anchor Tavern, 34 Park Street SE1 Tel: 0207-407 1577.
The George Inn, 77 Borough High Street SE1 Tel: 0207-407 2056.
The Old Operating Theatre, St Thomas's Street SE1 Tel: 0207-955 4791
Tue–Sun 10.00–16.00.

London Dungeon, 28 Tooley Street SE1   Tel: 0207-403 0606
Seven days a week 10.00–16.30. Admission charge.

22. Greenwich
Charing Cross Pier   Tel: 0207-987 1185 for sailing times.
Cutty Sark, King William Walk SE10   Tel: 0208-858 3445
Mon–Sat 10.00–18.00 (Oct–Mar 10.00–17.00), Sun 12.00–18.00.
Admission charge.
Royal Naval College, King William Walk SE10   Tel: 0208-858 2154
Seven days a week 14.30–16.45.
Queen's House, Romney Road SE10   Tel: 0208-858 4422
Seven days a week 10.00–17.00. Admission charge.

23. Pluckley
St Nicholas's Church, The Street, Pluckley, Kent
Seven days a week 10.00–16.00.
Blacksmith's Forge Tea Rooms, Smarden Road, Pluckley, Kent.
Black Horse Inn, The Street, Pluckley, Kent   Tel: 01233-840256.

24. A Gaggle of Ghosts
Westminster Abbey, Dean's Yard SW1
Seven days a week 8.00–18.00.
St Giles Cripplegate, EC2
Seven days a week 10.00–16.00.
Bruce Castle, Lordship Lane N17   Tel: 0208-808 8772
Wed–Sun 13.00–17.00.
St Mary's Church, Neasden Lane NW10
Seven days a week 10.00–16.00.
Hall Place, Bourne Road, Bexley, Kent   Tel: 01322-526574
Mon–Sat 10.00–16.30.
The Old Palace, Croydon, Surrey   Tel: 0208-688 2027
Tours only at certain times; phone for details.

Bibliography

There are many books that contain details of hauntings and many more about the history of London. I include here a list of books that have proved useful to me in researching this book and which I unreservedly recommend.

Abbott, G., *Ghosts of the Tower of London* (Hendon 1989)

Barker, Felix, & Silvester-Carr, Denise, *The Black Plaque Guide to London* (Constable 1987)

Begg, Paul, Fido, Martin & Skinner, Keith, *The Jack the Ripper A–Z* (Headline 1991)

Burger, Eugene, *Spirit Theatre* (Kaufman and Greenberg 1986)

Bushell, Peter, *London's Secret History* (Constable 1983)

Duncan, Andrew, *Village London* (New Holland Publishers (UK) Ltd 1997)

Duncan, Andrew, *Walking London* (New Holland Publishers (UK) Ltd, new edition 1999)

Encyclopaedia of Ghosts and Spirits (Guinness 1994)

Encyclopaedia of Magic and Superstition (Octopus 1974)

Forman, Joan, *Haunted Royal Homes* (Jarrold 1987)

Gibson, Peter, *The Capital Companion* (Webb and Bower 1985)

Green, Andrew, *Our Haunted Kingdom* (Fontana 1974)

Hole, Christine, *Haunted England* (Fitzhouse 1990)

Manchester, Sean, *The Highgate Vampire* (Gothic Press 1991)

Meller, Hugh, *London Cemeteries* (Gregg 1985)

The Unexplained File: Cult and Occult (Orbis 1985)

Murphy, Ruth, Whicelow, Clive, *Mysterious Wimbledon* (Enigma 1994)

Thurston Hopkins, R., *Cavalcade of Ghosts* (Worlds Work 1956)

Underwood, Peter, *Ghosts and How to See Them* (Anaya 1993)

Underwood, Peter, *Ghosts of Kent* (Meresborough 1985)

Underwood, Peter, *This Haunted Isle* (Javelin 1986)

Weinrob, Ben & Hibbert, Christopher (editors), *The London Encyclopaedia* (Macmillan 1983)

Ziegler, Philip, *The Black Death* (Penguin 1982)

Index